The Seven Key Aspects

of

TESTAMENTARY TRUSTS

View Legal

Matthew Burgess

Patrick Ellwood

National Library of Australia Cataloguing-in-Publication entry (pbk)

Author: Burgess, Matthew, author.
Title: The seven key aspects of testamentary trusts / Matthew Burgess, Patrick Ellwood
ISBN: 9781925181104 (paperback)
Subjects: Testamentary trusts—Australia.
Estate planning—Australia.
Other Authors/Contributors: Ellwood, Patrick, author.
Dewey Number: 346.94052

Important disclaimer

This book covers legal and technical issues in a general way. It is not designed to express opinions on specific cases. This book is intended for information purposes only and should not be regarded as legal advice. Further advice should be obtained before taking action on any issue dealt with in this publication.

Book design by Otto Dimitrijevics
Cover Design by Otto Dimitrijevics

Table of Contents

Introduction

Matthew Burgess, Patrick Ellwood, Naomi Arnold and Tara Lucke are co-founders, of View Legal.

Having previously founded Australia's first virtual law firm as a wholly owned subsidiary of one of the country's leading independent law firms, View Legal is results focused and passionate about delivering new solutions in a way that aligns with their 'SPS' – service and price satisfaction – guarantee.

As authors, Patrick and Matthew are recognised as experts in their fields, who constantly create innovative strategies for the growth, management and protection of wealth.

They are widely published across a range of topics including:

1. The Nine Steps to a Complete Estate Plan.
2. The Four Foundations of Business Succession.
3. Seven Essential Blue Journal Articles.
4. Inside Stories – the complete collection of blog posts (2010-2013)

Acknowledgements

This book has been based on material published by a number of leading lawyers at View Legal and, historically, the firm McCullough Robertson Lawyers. The assistance of all involved is gratefully acknowledged.

Important disclaimer

This book covers legal and technical issues in a general way. It is not designed to express opinions on specific cases. This book is intended for information purposes only and should not be regarded as legal advice. Further advice should be obtained before taking action on any issue dealt with in this publication.

Chapter 1

INTRODUCTION

Introduction

A TESTAMENTARY TRUST IS simply a trust established pursuant to a will. Most testamentary trusts are similar to 'normal' discretionary trusts established during the lifetime of a person, complete with classes of potential beneficiaries, extensive powers and unfettered discretions given as to distributions to the trustees of income and capital.

Trust overview

A trust is, in effect, simply a legal relationship where there is:

a a legal owner of property (the 'trustee')
b who holds the property ('trust property')
c for the benefit of others (the 'beneficiaries')
d pursuant to certain terms or rules ('trust deed').

Diagrammatically, the structure of a trust is represented below:

Figure 1.1

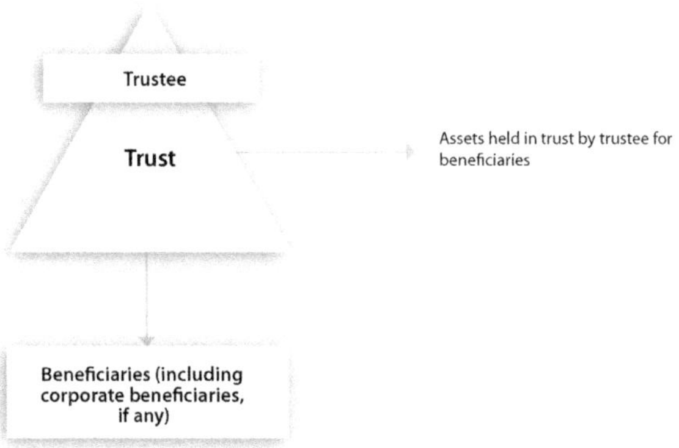

Trustee

The trustee is the legal owner of the property. The trustee will therefore have the ultimate control over the assets of the trust.

The trustee can be a company or one or more individuals. Where the trustee is a company, the directors of the company will have the day-to-day control of the trust.

As the shareholders of the company appoint the directors, the shareholders will have the ultimate control over the trust.

Despite this ultimate control, the shares in the trustee company will normally only be worth a nominal amount, regardless of the value of the assets in the trust that the trustee company controls.

The Office of State Revenue, in both Western Australia and Queensland, has the ability to attribute far greater value to the shares in the trustee company – based on the value of trust assets, rather than the value of the shares themselves. Therefore, in relation to shares in trustee companies for trusts in those states, care needs to be taken, from a stamp duty perspective.

Although the trustee is responsible for the day-to-day running of the trust, many trusts also have an '*appointor*' (also commonly known as a principal, guardian or nominator) who retains ultimate control over the trust. The appointor has the ability to appoint and remove the trustee at any time, and its consent may be required to make any amendments to the trust deed.

If the trust deed or will does not name an appointor, the existing trustee will usually have the power to appoint a new trustee.

Beneficiaries

The discretionary trust structure enables income that is earned by the trust to be distributed to the beneficiaries of the trust in such proportions as the trustee decides.

Normally, there are numerous beneficiaries set out – for example:, a mother and father; children and grandchildren; any brothers or sisters of any one mentioned before; any other trust in which any of these people are potential beneficiaries; any company in which any of these people hold any interest. These people are normally referred to as '*discretionary beneficiaries*'. The main reason for including a large number of discretionary beneficiaries is to allow the trustee maximum flexibility when distributing income.

The trustee is able to decide the proportions in which the income of the trust is distributed among these potential beneficiaries, on the basis of what would be appropriate, given the needs of the beneficiaries, and what is most tax effective in any given year.

One common strategy is to include a company as a potential beneficiary of the trust. As companies are currently taxed at a flat rate of

30% it can be an effective strategy to distribute income from the trust to the company so as to limit the overall tax paid by a family group.

Normally there will be one or two people who have an expectation of receiving income from the trust. These people are commonly referred to as the '*primary beneficiaries*'.

Most trusts set out who is to be entitled to the income of the trust if the trustee does not exercise its discretion to decide how to distribute the income. These are known as the '*default beneficiaries*'. Most trusts separately set out who are the default beneficiaries for any income that has not been distributed at the end of each year, and who are the default beneficiaries for capital upon the winding up of the trust. The default beneficiaries are often the same people as the primary beneficiaries.

Trust deed

Every trust is governed by a trust deed. This sets out how the trust must be run, what the trustees can do in running the trust and who the beneficiaries are. Discretionary trusts have been used as tax effective asset owning vehicles for a long time. Consequently, there are large numbers of trusts, governed by trust deeds that were drafted when the tax and trust laws were significantly different.

As mentioned above, testamentary trusts are established under a will, with the rules of the trust normally set out in the will itself.

It is necessary to review a trust deed periodically to ensure that it allows the trustees to operate the trust in the most tax effective way.

It is also important to review the terms of the trust deed carefully, with particular reference to issues such as:

a the vesting day (or ending day) of the trust. In all Australian states, except South Australia, a trust can last for a maximum periodof 80 years

b whether there is an '*appointor*'. As mentioned above, this person or entity has the ability to remove and appoint trustees at their total discretion

c. the powers the trustee has in relation to administering the trust. For example, trustees might not always be able to grant options in relation to trust property
d. what provisions apply in the event a trustee fails to make a distribution.

Testamentary trusts

A timeline of the administration of an estate and testamentary trustis summarised at figure 1.2.

Figure 1.2

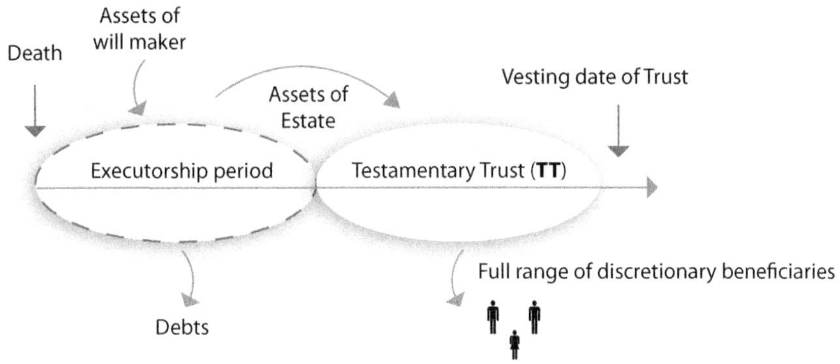

Essentially, the estate is administered by the executor, concluding with the designated assets or portions of the estate then held by the trustee of the testamentary trust.

Generally, testamentary trusts are seen as particularly useful in the following circumstances:

a to ensure concessional tax treatment is available to distributions of capital and income to infant beneficiaries

b to protect accumulated wealth from wastrel or spendthrift beneficiaries

c to provide for infant children and disabled beneficiaries

d to help protect inheritances from attack by the Family Court and trustees in bankruptcy

e to avoid an unintended loss by a beneficiary of agovernment sourced pension or other benefits (there is limited scope for this).

Testamentary trusts are often structured to limit the range of beneficiaries to 'lineal descendants', whereby the will maker restricts the discretionary powers of the trustee so they may only distribute income or capital (or both) to the will maker's children and grandchildren, excluding any spouse of the children and/or grandchildren.

Why use a lineal descendant trust? (LDT)

A lineal descendant testamentary trust is a trust established, in someone's will, for the benefit of their lineal descendants – children and grandchildren, and so on down the lineal family tree.

Many parents are concerned that the inheritance they leave to their children could end up in the hands of a son-in-law or daughter-in-law if their child's marriage were to break down. A properly drafted LDT can assist in keeping an inheritance out of the reach of the Family Court where a beneficiary is involved in a family law property dispute.

If a child receives an inheritance in their own name, that inheritance will generally be intermingled with the child's other assets (e.g. by paying off a mortgage) and will therefore become 'matrimonial property' available for distribution by the Family Court.

However, if each child receives their inheritance in a separate LDT, those assets can be kept apart and protected from direct distribution.

How successfully the assets are protected depends on how the will and LDT are drafted, and the circumstances at the time of drafting and when a relationship of a beneficiary breaks down.

Estate planning and asset protection

For those who have put in place 'asset protection' strategies or those who could be facing bankruptcy, receiving an inheritance can cause a problem. People in financially high-risk occupations such as professionals, business owners and company executives, will often prefer not to receive inherited assets in their own name.

If an estate is left to an individual absolutely then it is their property and can be jeopardised by their financial position at the time of the will maker's death, or at any time in the future. Should a person suffer matrimonial or financial misfortune, the testamentary trust provides a facility whereby the inheritance can be protected.

Tax planning

In Australia, death is not viewed as a tax planning strategy. It is, therefore, possible to draft a testamentary trust so as to ensure that any income allocated to minor children is not subject to the same tax rates as if it were a trust established during a person's lifetime. In particular, under a family trust created during a person's life, the first $400 distributed to a child is tax free but any further income is taxed at the highest rate, which in some circumstances can be as much as 66%.

Income derived by infant children via a testamentary trust however is assessed at the normal, individual adult rates – the first $24,000 (approximately) is tax free and the balance is taxed at marginal rates;for most families, this will mean significant tax planning opportunities.

Other benefits

In addition to the tax planning and asset protection benefits outlined above, appropriately structured testamentary trusts can also achieve numerous other objectives including:

a protecting assets from creditors, which can be a particularly important advantage where potential beneficiaries are company directors, business owners or professionals

b facilitating 'generation skipping', by ensuring that the majority of wealth passes to a will makers'grandchildren, as opposed to their children

c providing a structure within which it is possible to provide disproportionately for particular beneficiaries -for example, the trustees could have discretion to increase entitlements for those beneficiaries with special needs and decrease distributions to spendthrift or 'at risk' beneficiaries d creating the ability to structure multiple testamentary trusts under a single will, with each trust tailored to achieve particular objectives in relation to the intended beneficiaries of that trust.

Later chapters ofthis book will deal with all of the above issues in further detail and will consider in particular the following concepts:

a testamentary trusts and bankruptcy
b testamentary trusts and the family court
c protective trusts, other types of special testamentary trusts and practical considerations for testamentary trusts
d complex forms of testamentary trusts
e creative uses of testamentary trusts
f the taxation of testamentary trusts.

Chapter 2

TESTAMENTARY TRUSTS AND ASSET PROTECTION: PROTECTION FROM BANKRUPTCY

Introduction

ASSET PROTECTION STRATEGIES can be the single most important issue to consider in estate planning, particularly, where potential beneficiaries are in occupations, professional practice or business, or where there is a risk that a personal relationship of a beneficiary may degenerate in the future. Potential beneficiaries that fall into any of these 'at risk' categories will be exposed to losing assets, unless appropriate structures are put in place.

Against this background, the focus of this chapter is on the effective use of testamentary trusts to protect estates from insolvent beneficiaries.

What is asset protection?

BEFORE EXPLORING HOW testamentary trusts can be used to protect assets from insolvent beneficiaries, it is important to understand the broad principles of asset protection.

Generally, having 'asset protection' means being able to control assets or having access to benefits from assets that the relevant person does not legally own, so that if the person is sued, these assets will not be available to a successful plaintiff. Common examples include assets owned by a family company or trust and assets held by a spouse.

Asset protection also involves minimising exposure to the risk of losing assets and the risk of being sued.

For professionals such as accountants and lawyers, this normally means minimising the risk of a professional negligence suit by taking appropriate care when providing advice and seeking help from experts when necessary.

In the case of a manufacturer, for example, this includes having in place systems to minimise the chance of a faulty item being produced, completing orders and complying with contracts on time and having a safe working environment to minimise injuries to employees. As is often said:'prevention is better than cure'.

There are many ways in which a person can minimise exposure to risk, all of which are a form of asset protection. Broadly speaking, asset protection is optimised by having a number of layers of protection. For example:

a. first layer – ensure that therisk of liability is minimised by keeping up to date, seeking expert advice when required and taking care when providing advice or products
b. second layer – have adequate insurance cover
c. third layer – own, as opposed to benefit from,few or no assets.

Asset protection involves more than simply considering what will occur if a beneficiary is successfully sued. It must encompass protection of all of the person's assets, including business assets, personal assets, superannuation and future entitlements due to a relative's estate plan.

Broad principles

In any discussion of asset protection, a useful starting point is to outline the ideal position and then determine how easily it can be achieved, if at all.

A standard position in a typical 'mum and dad' family situation might be:

a there would be one 'high risk' person and one 'low risk' person
b the 'high risk' person would be the one involved in the operation of the business and would be the only company director, or 'at risk' professional,in the family. That person is, therefore, exposed to personal liability
c the 'high risk' spouse should not own or control any assets or wealth;neither should they be in a position where they may inherit wealth in their own name
d the 'low risk' spouse should own and/or control all assets and wealth. That person would not be exposed to the liabilities associated with directorship of a trading company, but may be a sole director and controller of a passive investment company or trustee of an investment trust with no trading operations.

This ideal position summarised above reflects the broad principles of:

a containing risks in limited liability entities
b keeping, moving or accumulating assets away from 'high risk' entities and into the hands of 'low risk' entities – including trusts, spouses and superannuation funds – and being careful that:

(i) the moving of assets must itself take account of bankruptcy and other 'claw back' rules (see below) and the revenue consequences of any transfers
(ii) the future receipt of assets – for example, from superannuation or under wills – must be anticipated and managed to keep assets away from 'high risk' entities and individuals at every juncture.

Sources of threats

The way in which testamentary trusts provide asset protection should be considered in the light of various potential sources of threat, including:

a the risk of a claim by a trustee in bankruptcy – for example, resulting from claims by creditors or litigants and claims against directors
b risks resulting from a marriage breakdown or breakdown in a de facto relationship
c risks arising following death or incapacity – for example, claims against the estate or assets passing to spendthrift beneficiaries who need 'protecting from themselves'
d business succession risks.

This chapter focuses solely on the role testamentary trusts can play in providing commercial levels of asset protection from bankruptcy.

Assets that can form part of a testamentary trust

Overview

Before a testamentary trust can be used to provide asset protection benefits, assets must firstly pass into the structure under a will, following the death of the will maker.

It is vital in any estate plan, from as early as possible in the process, to understand clearly which assets are regulated by the person's will and which assets need to be regulated utilising other strategies.

A brief summary of the main types of assets that do not pass pursuant to a person's will are set out in the table below.

Asset Type	Control	Documents Regulating
Joint Tenancy (as opposed to tenants in common)	Survivor	Position at law
Superannuation (binding nomination)	Member	Valid binding nomination
Superannuation (no binding nomination)	Fund trustee, post death	Trust Deed or Terms of Pension

Asset Type	Control	Documents Regulating
Discretionary Trust (individual trustee)	Appointor/Principal, or in the absence of both, surviving trustee. If no surviving trustee then legal personal representative of the (previously) surviving trustee	Trust Deed or *Trusts Act* 1973 (Qld) (**Trusts Act**)
Discretionary Trustee (corporate trustee)	Appointor/Principal or, in the absence of both, remaining directors of corporate trustee, subject to the shareholder's power to remove	Trust Deed or constitution for corporate trustee
Unit Trust	As above for discretionary trusts	Ultimate benefit in trust regulated by Trust Deed and unit holdings
Private Company	Director, subject to appointment by shareholders	Constitution or shareholders agreement. Transfer of shares may be pursuant to will depending on other documentation
Loan to Company or Trust	Lender or legal personal representative of Lender	Loan Agreement may override will
Business interests	Remaining business owners/trustee of will	Business Succession Agreement/Partnership Agreement

Asset Type	Control	Documents Regulating
Life Insurance	Policy owner or nominated beneficiary	Insurance Policy

The above table is not intended to be an exhaustive list of assets that fall outside a person's estate, but rather is designed to highlight the importance for clients of working with all their advisers, including their financial planner, lawyer, accountant and insurance broker, in devising a comprehensive estate plan.

There are increasing numbers of examples where will makers' objectives are not met. This can be due to the failure to establish legal ownership, or because will makers' structure their affairs before taking advice about the distribution and preservation of assets upon death. Similarly, there seems to be an increasing number of disgruntled beneficiaries who readily seek to attribute blame when unintended consequences arise.

Estate planning

An important aspect of any structuring of personal assets, to ensure protection from bankruptcy,is to make sure that the following components complement each other:

a. wills (incorporating testamentary trusts)
b. enduring powers of attorney
c. passing on control of entities.

Depending upon the approach adopted, regarding the structuring of assets, there could be very little to be dealt with under an individual'swill.

Where a married couple structure their assets in such a way that the party with a low risk profile owns the bulk of the assets, it is very important to ensure that their wills are drafted so that their prior good planning is not undone if the 'low-risk' spouse predeceases the spouse with a high risk profile.

Rather than having assets pass to the partner with exposure, they should generally be transferred, under the will, to a testamentary trust (to be discussed below), where the surviving spouse is a potential beneficiary, with others, and does not have control of the trust.

The issue of control, which is a perennial issue in the estateplanning context, is vital where bankruptcy is a concern. In addition to emotive issues such as whether the surviving spouse will 'do the right thing' by other beneficiaries, the risks of bankruptcy might make their involvement as a trustee inappropriate.

There might be similar issues in terms of children's exposure if they are in the high-risk categories outlined above. Furthermore, the children might be unwilling to take on the responsibility, or the surviving partner might have no confidence that the children will act in their best interests. It is a dilemma not easily resolved without a methodical approach by the client and their advisers.

Risk of claims by a trustee in bankruptcy

WHERE AN INDIVIDUAL or entity is involved in a profession or conducting a business, claims against the individual or entity by creditors or potential litigants can expose all of the assets held by that individual or entity.

The possibilities for litigation and claims by creditors against individuals to arise (and, therefore, the potential for bankruptcy to occur) are numerous and include:

a claims against a business by its suppliers
b product liability of manufacturing businesses
c professional negligence claims against professionals – for example, doctors, lawyers, accountants and financial advisers
d general negligence claims – for example, operation of a motor vehicle causing personal or property damage.

There are also numerous potential risks of claims being made against directors of companies, including personal liability for:

a the company's debts incurred in insolvent trading
b some tax obligations of the company
c unpaid employees' superannuation deductions
d an ever-widening statutory liability, where directors are personally liable for the company's actions. Many State and Federal Acts impose this personal liability – one example is Workplace Health and Safety legislation
e negligence
f guarantees.

Even relatively passive assets can result in litigation against the owner, which brings with it the potential for bankruptcy. For example, a person who owns an investment property in their own name can be personally sued if a tenant trips and sustains an injury on the property. As mentioned above, insurance is, of course, a critical risk minimisation strategy in this case.

It is, therefore, vital to ensure that as many assets as possible are quarantined from an 'at risk' individual or entity to avoid them being exposed to potential claims against that individual or entity. It is also vital to ensure that assets with high-risk exposure are quarantined from all other assets to limit the potential exposure to the value of those assets.

Movement into bankruptcy

Even if an individual or entity has caused litigation to arise, a number of things must happen before a trustee in bankruptcy becomes involved. In summary, the steps are as follows:

a there must be a debt
b if that debt is a judgement debt, there will have been a claim that has been successfully prosecuted in the courts
c there must have been a failure to meet that debt
d the creditor must have then sought to appoint a trustee in bankruptcy to the debtor's estate.

Depending on the circumstances, other arrangements might be considered to avoid the appointment of a trustee in bankruptcy. For example, the debtor might enter into an informal agreement with creditors, or enter into arrangements under Parts IX or X *Bankruptcy Act 1966* (Cth) (**Bankruptcy Act**).

A discussion of these various arrangements and options is outside the scope of this book; the focus here is the worst-case scenario, where a trustee in bankruptcy is appointed. However, the principles of protecting assets from exposure to claims against individuals are also relevant in the case of a scheme of arrangement.

Section 120, 121 and 122 'claw back' rules

In considering claims that might be brought by a trustee in bankruptcy, it is relevant to bear in mind the voidable transaction provisions in the Bankruptcy Act. These provisions, often referred to as 'claw back' provisions, enable the trustee in bankruptcy to trace and reclaim assets that were transferred prior to a person becoming bankrupt.

In particular, a transfer can be overturned, subject to certain exclusions:

a if the transfer took place within two years before the commencement of the bankruptcy, where no consideration was paid or where consideration was less than market value (section 120(3) Bankruptcy Act) – or four years for related entities
b if the transfer took place within five years before the commencement of the bankruptcy and, at the time of the transfer, the person was insolvent, where no consideration was paid or where consideration was less than market value (section 120(1) Bankruptcy Act)
c if the transfer took place within six months before the commencement of the bankruptcy, the transfer is to a creditor, the creditor obtains a preference, priority or advantage over other creditors and at the time of the transfer the transferor was insolvent (section 122 Bankruptcy Act)
d at any time where the main purpose in making the transfer is to prevent the transferred property from becoming divisible, or to hinder or to delay the process of making property available for division, among creditors (section 121(1) Bankruptcy Act).

As the commencement of the bankruptcy may be dated from the first act of bankruptcy within the six months before a relevant petition was presented, up to a further six months can be added to these periods of 'claw back'.

It is significant to note that, if sections 120 and 121 Bankruptcy Act void (claw back) the transfer of property, there is a requirement to pay to the transferee the consideration (if any) that they had paid.

These provisions pose a potential threat to the whole strategy of accumulating assets in the hands of 'low risk' entities, where value must be 'moved' (a financial contribution) to that 'low risk' entity.

Relevantly, however, in the context of testamentary trusts:

a transfers that take place, under a will, on death are not subject to claw back

b subject to comments set out below, the bankruptcy of a beneficiary of a testamentary trust does not jeopardise the assets of the trust.

Bankruptcy issues with testamentary trusts

Vesting of property upon bankruptcy

Generally, the property of the bankrupt vests in the trustee in bankruptcy as, and from, the commencement of the bankruptcy.

However, subject to the comments below, the property of the bankrupt does not include the assets of a trust (including a testamentary trust) of which they are a discretionary object. The primary reason for this is that none of the beneficiaries of a testamentary trust has any defined interest in the trust assets, but merely the right to have the trust administered in accordance with the terms of the trust established under the deed or will (*Gartside v Inland Revenue Commissioners* [1968] AC 553).

Therefore, if a beneficiary becomes bankrupt, the assets of the testamentary trust will not be available to their creditors unless the trustee makes a distribution to that beneficiary.

This general position is subject to a number of possible exceptions, including:

a flow through of income
b exposing the assets of the testamentary trust
c 'beneficiary loan accounts' or other debts owed by the trustee to a bankrupt beneficiary
d where the bankrupt is a default beneficiary
e where the 'at risk' beneficiary is the appointor/principal
f where the 'at risk' beneficiary is the trustee.

Each of these issues will be dealt with in turn below, before the implications of the *Australian Securities and Investments Commission In the Matter ofRichstar Enterprises Pty Ltd v Carey (No. 6)* [2006] FCA 814 (**Richstar**) decision are considered in detail.

Flow through of income

Income derived by a testamentary trust will usually flow through to the beneficiaries by force of tax pressure. This is to ensure that the trustee is not assessed at the top marginal tax rate under section 99A *Income Tax Assessment Act* 1936 (**ITAA 1936**) on any undistributed income.

Beneficiaries will be presently entitled to income, which is appointed or applied to them by the trustee. Clearly, where a beneficiary who has a vested interest because the trustee exercises its discretion to vest income (or indeed capital) in the beneficiary, that interest will be exposed to a claim against the beneficiary.

A simple solution would be for the trustee to exercise its discretionary power to distribute the share of the income, for any year where a beneficiary is bankrupt, to beneficiaries who are themselves not at risk.

Other possiblesolutions include:

a establishing separate or sub-trusts in relation to income to which beneficiaries other than the bankrupt are presently entitled. In either case, the amounts distributed to those trusts will be liabilities in which the trustee in bankruptcy will have no priority

b ensuring that the terms of the testamentary trust prohibit the trustees from distributing income and capital to the 'at risk' beneficiary.

Exposing the assets of the trust

It is important to remember that using a testamentary trust does not magically confer protection on the assets of the trust. The assets of the trust can easily be exposed within the trust environment – in particular, where the trustees carry on a business or apply the assets to other high-risk activities.

Ideally, therefore, testamentary trusts should be utilised solely for passive investments or, alternatively (as mentioned above), sub-trusts or separate structures should be used to quarantine higher risk activities.

Beneficiary loan accounts

The balance of 'beneficiary loan accounts',which have been built up as a result of tax distributions not being matched by cash payments out of the trust, should be reviewed regularly.

Any credit beneficiary loan account is an asset of the beneficiary, and thus exposed to any claim brought against the beneficiary. It is important to ensure that trustees do not create beneficiary loan accounts in beneficiaries with a high level of exposure.

It is also unwise to have 'at risk' beneficiaries lending back distributions received to the trust;this also leads to the creation (and accumulation) of a loan account in favour of the beneficiary in the trust.

It is important to ensure that beneficiaries with a level of exposure deal properly with loan accounts on an ongoing basis, particularly with regard to claw back provisions of the Bankruptcy Act, set out above, which could mean that the assets of the trust remain exposed four years or more after a beneficiary gifts a previously created loan account back to the trust.

Default beneficiaries

Most testamentary trusts include default provisions, in relation to both income and capital. That is, if the trustee fails to exercise effectively its discretion to distribute income in any year, or capital on the trust vesting date, the trustee will be deemed to hold the undistributed income or capital for nominated default beneficiaries.

Some commentators have argued that the interest of these default beneficiaries constitutes property that may vest in the trustee in bankruptcy if a default beneficiary is declared bankrupt.

It has generally been argued that the interest of default beneficiaries is of a different character from that of a discretionary object and may well be property of a bankrupt (*Dwyer v Ross* (1992) 34 FCR 463) (**Dwyer v Ross**).

However, it has also been argued that the interests of takers in default do not have a vested interest in the assets of the trust until the trust vests, and until that event occurs, the assets of the trust have not been the subject of an effective appointment. That is, such interests can be deferred or taken away at any time prior to vesting or termination of the trust and, accordingly, such interests are 'mere expectancies' in respect of property that is not capable of vesting in a trustee in bankruptcy.

The preferred position adopted by the cases (despite the *Richstar* decision) remains that a default beneficiary does not have an interest in trust assets that amounts to property that is attackable by a trustee in bankruptcy.

This said, it is always appropriate, when establishing a testamentary trust, to consider carefully who should be nominated as the default beneficiaries to ensure that the assets of the trust do not become unnecessarily exposed to claims against those beneficiaries if the law in this area changes.

Powers of appointor/principal

Many testamentary trusts create a position for an appointor or principal who generally has the power of removal and appointment of the trustee.

A question that often arises is: if a principal/appointor is subsequently declared bankrupt, is their power of appointment a 'property' which vests in and can be exercised by the trustee in bankruptcy?

The property of a bankrupt, which is available for distribution to creditors, includes 'the capacity to exercise, and to take proceedings for exercising, all such powers in, over or in respect of property as might have been exercised by the bankrupt for his own benefit…' (see section 116(1)(b) Bankruptcy Act).

However, it has been held that the right of a bankrupt to exercise a power of appointment under a discretionary trust is not property of the bankrupt (*Re Burton; ex parte Wily v Burton* (1994) 126 ALR 557).

Further, the decision in *Dwyer v Ross* suggests that a trustee in bankruptcy cannot compel the trustee of a trust to exercise the trustee's discretion in favour of a bankrupt beneficiary. To do so could be construed as a breach of the trustee's duty to the solvent beneficiaries of the trust. It would be against the interests of the beneficiaries as a whole to exercise the power in that way. As a practical matter, however, if a trustee in bankruptcy purports to act in that way, the beneficiary and trustee is left to take action against the trustee which, on a number of levels (not least of which being financial capacity),might not be possible.

Again, however, with reference to the principles following *Richstar*(outlined below) it is still prudent to ensure that:

a there are at least two persons filling the appointor/principal role and they must act jointly
b any appointor/principal can resign
c any appointor/principal is automatically removed if declared bankrupt.

Powers of trustees

Similar to those of an appointor or principal, the trustee's powers may be available for distribution for creditors and therefore a similar approach to the appointor/principal should be adopted to minimise the risk for a trustee of the testamentary trust.

Especially in circumstances where a beneficiary under a testamentary trust is also appointed as a trustee, it would be sensible to appoint multiple trustees to act jointly with the beneficiary; these may include a:

a family member
b family friend
c trustee company,, or
d a combination of the above.

Alternatively, as mentioned above, in relation to an appointor/principal, the testamentary trust may contain a clause that automatically removes trustees if they are declared bankrupt.

An example of how this type of clause can be drafted is set out below.

The powers of the Trustee (or each Trustee if there is more than one) cease on:

a *death*
b *the loss of lawful capacity through age, accident, or illness (evidence of which is by certificate of a registered medical practitioner)*
c *the Trustee committing an 'act of bankruptcy' within the meaning of section 40 Bankruptcy Act 1966 (Cth) (***Bankruptcy Act***) (excluding section 40(b) Bankruptcy Act)*
d *a sequestration order being made against the Trustee under section 43 Bankruptcy Act*
e *the Trustee presenting a declaration of the Trustee's intention to present a debtor's petition, under section 54A Bankruptcy Act*
f *the Trustee presenting a petition against themselves under section 55 Bankruptcy Act*
g *the Trustee entering into a part X personal insolvency agreement under the Bankruptcy Act*
h *the Trustee entering into a part IX debt agreement under the Bankruptcy Act*
i *a receiver, receiver and manager, or controller (as defined in section 9 Corporations Act 2001 (Cth) (***Corporations Act***)) being appointed to all or any part of the Trust Fund*
j *an administrator of the Trustee being appointed under section 436A or section 436C Corporations Act*
k *an order for the winding up of the Trustee being made under section 233, section 459A, section 459B or section 461 Corporations Act*
l *a resolution being passed for the winding up of the Trustee under section 491 Corporations Act*

m *the Trustee being deregistered under section 601AB or section 601AC Corporations Act*

n *the holder of a mortgage or charge taking, or appointing an agent to take, possession of all or any part of the Trust Fund*

o *any application being made for an order under the Family Law Act 1975 (Cth) (Family Law Act) in respect of the Trustee*

p *the Trustee suffering a relationship 'breakdown' within the meaning of the Family Law Act*

q *the Trustee separating from their spouse within the meaning of 'separation' under the Family Law Act.*

The Richstar decision and beyond

ALTHOUGH *RICHSTAR* DID not directly refer to testamentary trusts, the 2006 decision set alarm bells ringing because of its redefinition of established discretionary trust principles – principles that form the basis of the majority of testamentary trusts.

Background

The *Richstar* case stemmed from the litigation surrounding the failed Westpoint group. The Federal Court had already appointed receivers to the property of several directors and companies of the failed group. ASIC sought to have the meaning of 'property' (for the purposes of it being available for distribution amongst creditors) extended to include property held by a third party on trust for a defendant, including where the defendant was a general beneficiary of a discretionary trust.

The key issue considered by the decision was the definition of 'property' in section 9 *Corporations Act 2001* (**Corporations Act**). Section 9 provides that property 'means any legal or equitable estate or interest (whether present or future and whether vested or contingent) in real or personal property of any description and includes a thing in action'.

What happened?

The Court held that some of the defendants had 'at least a contingent interest' in the trust property, which was sufficient for the property to be available to the receivers. A contingent interest was found to arise where 'the trustee is effectively the alter ego of the relevant beneficiary or otherwise subject to his or its effective control'.

Although this was not the full order sought by ASIC, the decision challenged the traditional view that a beneficiary of a discretionary trust has a mere 'expectancy', which is not sufficient to constitute 'property' that is available to creditors.

Exhaustive v non-exhaustive trusts

The Court held that the difference between 'exhaustive' and 'non-exhaustive' discretionary trusts was important.

Exhaustive trusts

Under an 'exhaustive' trust, the trust deed requires the trustee to distribute all of the income after each defined period.

Where an exhaustive trust has a closed class of beneficiaries, the beneficiaries, as a group, can direct the trustee how to deal with the property, and can require that the legal interest in the property be transferred to them.

Non-exhaustive trusts

Under a 'non-exhaustive' trust deed, the trustee can distribute the trust income however they see fit, whether that is a distribution of some, none, or all of the trust income.

Furthermore under a non-exhaustive trust deed, even a closed class of beneficiaries, acting together, cannot direct the trustee how to deal with the trust property.

Richstar held that 'in the ordinary case the beneficiary of a discretionary trust, other than perhaps the sole beneficiary of an exhaustive trust, does not have an equitable interest in the trust income or property which would fall within even the most generous definition of 'property' in section 9 Corporations Act'.

However, the Court went on to 'distinguish the "ordinary case" from the case in which the beneficiary effectively controls the trustee's power of selection', in which case, 'there is something which is akin to a proprietary interest in the beneficiary'.

Issues not considered

Somewhat surprisingly, the judgement did not address whether any of the trusts in question had default beneficiaries, even though default beneficiaries have long been regarded as perhaps having a legal interest in the trust property. Further, although some significance was given to the identity of the appointor, no mention was made of previous cases, which have held that an appointor's power of appointment is not 'property' for the purposes of the Bankruptcy Act.

Effect of Richstar

On its face, the *Richstar* decision appears to support the position that discretionary trust assets cannot be regarded as the 'property' of a person merely because that person is a beneficiary, trustee, director or shareholder of a trustee company, or an appointor. However, certain combinations of these roles might be sufficient to trigger a finding of effective control and hence an interest in 'property'. The distinction between the effect of each role individually and the effect of a combination of roles was not discussed in any detail in the case.

For many years, the Family Court has been able to 'look through' formal trust structures to decide who has de facto ownership of trust property. The decision in *Richstar* was significant because it was the first time that a beneficiary's interest in a discretionary trust had been held,potentially, to amount to a form of property in a commercial situation.

The decision in *Richstar* considered a number of Family Court cases in concluding that it was appropriate to look beyond the structure of the different legal entities involved (including lifting the corporate veil) to determine whether the relevant person could be said to have had effective control of the assets in question, and therefore some form of contingent interest.

The Court considered the likelihood that a beneficiary who controlled the trustee's power of selection would have exercised that power in their own favour. In this regard, it was held that 'where a discretionary trust is controlled by a trustee who is in truth the alter ego of a beneficiary, then at the very least a contingent interest may be identified because "it is as good as certain" that the beneficiary will receive the benefits of distributions either of income or capital or both.'

What does this mean for discretionary trusts?

The decision in *Richstar*represented a significant departure from the traditional view of discretionary trusts, but it was far from conclusive. As the case involved an interlocutory application in relation to a specific provision of the Corporations Act, its application was, and arguably still is, limited to similar fact scenarios. It is also worth remembering that this was an interim decision to preserve the trust assets held. Whether the assets could in fact be distributed to creditors, was not considered.

The main concern is that, if this approach is accepted and adopted generally within the context of appointing receivers, it could pave the way for trust assets to be available, for example, to trustees in bankruptcy or to company liquidators. If this were to happen, maintaining 'control' over a trustee would come at the significant price of reduced asset protection.

Cases since Richstar

It is also important to remember that the '*Richstar* decision' was only a single judge interim decision. While the judge is now the Chief Justice of the High Court, the decision itself has not yet been followed or applied by any other judges and could still be challenged in the future.

Furthermore in *Public Trustee v Smith* [2008] NSWCA 397 (**Smith**) there is some indication of the likely scope of the *Richstar* decision. The key issue in Smith was whether property that was owned by a discretionary trust could be considered as being owned by a person, who was the sole shareholder and director of the corporate trustee, to enable the assets to be gifted via that person's will.

The Court made a clear distinction between actual ownership and effective ownership and concluded that the will maker was not the actual (beneficial) owner of the trust assets. In relation to *Richstar*, it was noted by the Court in that case:

'Did not say that it followed from the defendant's position as beneficiaries of discretionary trusts and their control of the trustees that this amounted to actual ownership as distinct from effective control'.

In *Smith*, the Judge also confirmed:

'I do not understand ASIC v Carey (No. 6) (i.e. Richstar) to establish that because a beneficiary of a discretionary trust controls the appointment or removal of the trustee, or controls the exercise of the trustee's power and can appoint trust property to himself or herself, that the holder of such a power is the beneficial owner of the trust property irrespective of the terms of the trust deed'.

The above reasoning in *Smith* was applied by the same judge in a subsequent 2008 case.

Do discretionary trusts and testamentary trusts have a future?

For the time being, the benefits of discretionary trusts and testamentary trusts are generally still sufficient to make them the preferred structures for asset protection purposes.

That said, the issues and questions raised in *Richstar* remain significant and should be taken into account when thinking about structuring and establishing testamentary trusts.

Issues to consider when establishing a testamentary trust

DESPITE BEING HANDED down in 2006, the *Richstar* decision has remained topical and relevant, the overriding principle of the case being that anyone considering using a trust, or a testamentary trust for that matter, should review as many of the different aspects of the structure as possible.

The issues that should be considered when establishing the structure and control of a testamentary trust are:

a Who is the trustee of the trust? If the trustee ceases to act, do their powers pass to anyone else, and if so, to whom?
b Is the trustee an individual or a company?
c If the trustee is a company, who are its directors?
d Is there a default distribution of the income and capital of the trust to certain beneficiaries?
e Does the trust deed restrict the range of beneficiaries who can receive income or capital distributions?
f Does the trustee need consent or approval of any other person for distribution?
g Does the trustee effectively or practically control the trust in an unfettered way?
h Does the trustee exercise its powers independently or are they controlled or subject to approval by any other person or entity?
i Is the trustee a beneficiary of the trust?
j Can a beneficiary or a class of beneficiaries control the actions of the trustee?
k Can beneficiaries be removed or added, and if so by whom?
l Is there any risk that the trustee might be seen simply as the 'alter ego' of some other person?

m Does someone – for example, an appointor, guardian, principal, have the power to unilaterally change the trustee?

n If there is an appointor, is the role automatically terminated on certain events – for example, death, bankruptcy?

o If the appointor ceases to act, do their powers pass to anyone else, and if so, to whom?

p If there is more than one appointor, must they act jointly?

q Is the appointor a beneficiary of the trust?

r Will the trust own more than one asset class?

s For an existing trust, has there been a pattern of income or capital distributions to 'at risk' individuals associated with the trust?

t For an existing trust, have there been variations to the deed, following establishment,which have an impact on the overall control of the trust?

Chapter 3

TESTAMENTARY TRUSTS AND PROTECTION FROM FAMILY PROPERTY CLAIMS: IS IT POSSIBLE?

Introduction

As mentioned in Chapter 2, asset protection strategies and the use of testamentary trusts are important issues to consider in estate planning, particularly where there is a risk that a personal relationship of a beneficiary mightdegenerate in the future. Potential beneficiaries whofall into any of these 'at risk' categories will be exposed to losing assets, unless appropriate structures are put in place.

A significant attraction of excluding spouses as potential beneficiaries is the perception that it is more difficult for an excluded spouse to argue before the Family Court that the assets of the testamentary trust should be considered as anything other than a financial resource.

Recent years have been a turbulent time for the controllers of trusts and their advisers. Some of the developments that have challengedthe effectiveness of trust structures (including testamentary trusts) are:

a amendments to bankruptcy legislation to widen the situations in which trust assets might be exposed in the event of an individual associated with the trust becoming bankrupt

b continuing attempts (which to date have been unsuccessful) by trustees in bankruptcy to argue that the power of appointment over trust assets is of itself an asset of a bankrupt person capable of being exercised by the trustee in bankruptcy

c numerous changes to the application of the Division 7A tax regime to capture and tax arrangements where unpaid present entitlements have arisen following a distribution from a discretionary trust

d the *Richstar* decision, which called into question the level of asset protection a discretionary trust can provide if a controller of a trust personally becomes bankrupt. The *Richstar* decision arguably took on further significance when the presiding judge,

Justice French, subsequently became Chief Justice of the High Court

e the Government's decision,in late 2008,to abolish the capital gains tax exemption for trust cloning, which stripped the owners of many family trusts of the ability to restructure their trusts to achieve asset protection or succession planning objectives

f thedecisions in *Commissioner of Taxation v Bamford* [2010] HCA 10(**Bamford**), *Colonial First State Investments Limited v Commissioner of Taxation* [2011] FCA 16(**Colonial**) and*Commissioner of Taxation v David Clark; Commissioner of Taxation v Helen Clark* [2011] FCAFC 5(**Clark**)and subsequent Australian Taxation Office (ATO) and Government responses.

While all of the above issues have required (in some instances, significant) additional planning, for a combination of reasons, family discretionary trusts and testamentary trusts are still often viewed as the structures of choice for many business owners and private investors. In recent times, however, many advisers and clients have, perhaps unnecessarily, lost faith in the ability of trusts to protect assets in the event of a marriage breakdown.

Arguably, the most significant cause of this lack of confidence in trusts is the High Court decision of *Kennon v Spry*[2008] HCA 56(**Kennon v Spry**), on the basis that the decision in that case appeared to alter the longstanding principles relating to the asset protection advantages of trusts in the context of a marriage breakdown.

This chapter considers:

a the Family Courts' powers to deal with inheritances

b the consequences of the decision in *Kennon v Spry*

c discussion about the treatment of family trust and testamentary trust assets in a relationship breakdown, and the distinction between assets forming part of the pool of property or being treated as a financial resource

d the application of these principles in recent decisions concerning family trusts and testamentary trusts

e. some practical recommendations when dealing with trusts in the context of estate planning and structuring clients' affairs
f. whether a trust can still be an effective tool to protect assets and inheritances from exposure to relationship breakdowns.

The Family Courts' power to deal with inheritances

The meaning of 'property' in the Family Law Act 1975 (Cth) (Family Law Act)

In general terms,the starting point of a property division is to determinethe nature of the assets and liabilities of the parties to the marriage, and to classify those assets and liabilities as either property of the parties or a financial resource or, potentially, neither. If a court determines, as part of this process, that assets fall under the definition of a financial resource (as opposed to being the property of the parties), then those assets cannot be divided between the parties under a court order.

The table below provides a diagrammatic summary of the options available to the court when dealing with assets of the marriage:

Not property or a financial resource	Is a financial resource	Is property but only a portion represents property of the marriage	Is property and 100% should be treated as property of the marriage
←			→

The Family Law Act defines 'property' as '*property to which those parties are, or that party is, as the case may be, entitled, whether in possession or reversion*'. If an asset is 'property' of a party to a marriage, the Family Law Act confers a wide power on the court to vary the legal interests in the property and to make orders for a settlement of property in substitution for any interest in the property.

The definition of 'property' in the Family Law Act can be contrasted with the definition under the Bankruptcy Act, which states that 'property' is *'real or personal propertyof every description... and includes any estate, interest or profit, whether present or future, vested or contingent, arising out of or incident to any such real or personal property'.*

The Family Courts' treatment of inheritances

The question of whether an inheritance will be treated as property of the parties or a financial resource will depend on the circumstances of the relevant case. Where an inheritance has been received by a party absolutely (i.e. not via a testamentary trust), the courts have placed weight on the timing of the inheritance in the context of the relationship breakdown.

Generally speaking, the principles from the cases indicate that if the inheritance is received near the commencement of a marriage, then the normal rules relating to assessing contributions by the parties will apply.

Where the inheritance is received near the end of the relationship or after separation and the other party has made minimal contribution towards the inheritance, it will generally be excluded from the property pool.

In the 2010 decision of *Mistle and Mistle*[2010] FamCA 29 (**Mistle and Mistle**), the husband received an inheritance of $9.5 million after the parties had separated from their 23-year marriage. The property of the marriage at the time of separation was approximately $4 million.

The Court excluded the inheritance from the property pool and treated it as a financial resource of the husband, on the basis that:

a the inheritance was received after separation of the parties
b the wife had not made any contribution towards the inheritance
c there was sufficient property in the marital pool to achieve a just and equitable settlement for the wife.

In contrast with *Mistle and Mistle*, the earlier decisions of *James and James*[1978] FLC 90-487 and *Bonnici and Bonnici* [1992] FLC 92-272 indicate the Courts' approach where the spouse has made a contribution towards the inheritance and there are insufficient assets in the marital pool.

In *James and James*, the parties had lived for 13 years in a large home on the husband's father's property. During this time the husband had assisted his father with the operation of the property, with the expectation that, in due course, the land would pass to him under his father's estate. Throughout that time, the wife had also contributed to the running of the property. After the separation but before the property settlement proceedings, the husband's father died, leaving the husband a substantial inheritance.

The Full Court held, in making an adjustment of property in favour of the wife, that in the context of the expectations of both the husband and the wife that they would receive the propertyin the fullness of time (albeit in the husband's name), the inheritance should be considered as property of the parties.

In *Bonnici and Bonnici*,the Full Court of the Family Court considered the treatment of an inheritance received approximately six months before the parties' separation from their 20-year marriage.

The Court stated:

'A property does not fall into a protected category merely because it is an inheritance. On the other hand, if there are ample funds from which an appropriate property settlement can be made and a just result arrived at, then the fact of a recently acquired inheritance would normally be treated as an entitlement of the party in question. The other party cannot be regarded as contributing significantly to an inheritance received very late in the relationship and certainly not after it has terminated, except in very unusual circumstances...'

In this case, the inheritance received by the husband was largely comprised of a property upon which the parties' restaurant business had been conducted. The property and business were sold after the death of the husband's mother, with the net proceeds from the property divided between the husband and his sister.

The Full Court found that the wife clearly made substantial contributions to the restaurant business (including working without wages and her homemaking contributions), which justified including the inheritance in the property pool to achieve a just and equitable distribution.

In relation to a prospective inheritance not yet received, the Family Court has held in *White & Tulloch v White*[1995] FamCA 127(**White & Tulloch v White**)that a prospective inheritance was not a financial resource. The Court found that:

'An expectancy could not be said to be a financial resource, that term connoting some degree of entitlement to, control over, or relative certainty of receipt of property...the will is a mere expression of intention at the time it is made and may be freely revoked or altered and that it has no legal effect until the death of the testator...'

In this matter, the husband had asserted that due to the close relationship between the wife and her mother, the wife was highly likely to inherit half of the mother's estate, which was worth at least $1.2 million at the time of the proceedings.

The Court provided some guidance in relation to the circumstances when a prospective inheritance may be relevant:

'We do not consider there is any absolute rule. The ultimate criterion is whether the evidence is, or may be, relevant to the just and equitable process under s 79. An expectancy of inheritance will not be relevant in many s 79 proceedings. In the end, relevance must depend upon the nature of the claims being put forward and the facts of the particular case ....

... In a case where the testator had already made a will favourable to the party but no longer had testamentary capacity and there was evidence of his or her likely impending death in circumstances where there may be a significant estate, and where there was a connection to s 75(2) factors, it would be shutting one's eyes to realities to treat that as irrelevant. On the other hand, the bald assertion that one of the parties has an elderly relative who has property and is or is likely to benefit that party is so speculative that it would be inappropriate to contemplate it as relevant in a s 79 determination, it being too remote to affect the justice and equity of the case in any worthwhile way'.

The Family Courts' powers to deal with trust assets

THE ABOVE SUMMARY of the Family Courts' powers to deal with inheritances does not consider an inheritance received by a party to a marriage through a testamentary trust. It is, therefore, relevant to consider the Family Courts' powers in relation to trusts generally, in order to understand the exposure of assets in a testamentary trust on a relationship breakdown.

Asset protection principles relating to trusts

The asset protection typically understood to be afforded by trusts is derived from the longstanding view that a mere discretionary beneficiary of a trust does not have a proprietary interest in a trust's assets, and the main right of a discretionary beneficiary is limited to enforcing due administration by the trustee. Consequently, it is difficult to value this right when the beneficiary has no present entitlement to the trust's assets and mightnever have entitlement to any part of the income or capital of the discretionary trust.

While this has been the accepted view for hundreds of years, recent decisions in Australia potentially undermine the level of asset protection afforded by trusts. The high profile decision of *Richstar*(-mentioned earlier) considered whether a beneficiary can have a proprietary interest in the assets of a trust where that beneficiary has 'effective control' over the trust.

In*Richstar*, the Court held that some of the defendants had 'at least a contingent interest' in the trust property, which was sufficient for the property to be potentially available to the receivers. A contingent interest was found to arise where 'the trustee is effectively the alter ego of the relevant beneficiary or otherwise subject to his or its effective control'. Although the Court did not allow the full order sought by the ASIC, the decision challenged the traditional view that a beneficiary of a discretionary trust has no more than a mere 'expectancy', which, of itself is not sufficient to constitute 'property' thatis available to creditors.

For completeness, it should be noted that*Richstar* was a decision about proprietary interests in a bankruptcy context. As the focus of this chapter is on the proprietary interest of a beneficiary of a trust in the context of the Family Law Courts, the *Richstar*decision will not be discussed further.

Kennon v Spry

In 1968, the husband settled a discretionary trust named the ICF Spry Trust, of which he was both the trustee and settlor. The eligible beneficiaries consisted of the 'standard' range of beneficiaries typically found in a discretionary trust, including the husband, any spouse of the husband, the husband's issue, his siblings, their spouses and their issue, and charitable beneficiaries.

In 1978, the husband and the wife married and they subsequently had four daughters.

In 1983, the husband varied the trust deed by excluding himself as a beneficiary and appointing the wife as trustee on his death or resignation. As a result, the husband ceased to be a potential beneficiary. It was understood that this variation was madepredominantly for land tax purposes.

In December 1998, at a time when the wife argued the relationship was starting to strain, the husband executed a further deed of variation, which excluded his wife as a capital beneficiary.

During the course of 2002, the husband established a discretionary trust for each of the four daughters of the marriage, of which he was the initial trustee and was later the joint trustee with a Mr Edwin Philip Kennon. As trustee of the ICF Spry Trust, the husband then distributed the capital and income of that trust equally between the four children's trusts.

Following the couple's separation and subsequent divorce, the wife sought orders from the Court to setaside the distributions from the ICF Spry Trust to the children's trusts, arguing that the pool of assets for distribution should include the ICF Spry Trust's assets and the income distributed to the children's trusts.

The primary question before the Court was whether the pool of assets for distribution on the property settlement should comprise the assets of the ICF Spry trust. The wife argued that the pool should include the assets in the children's trusts, while the husband alleged that neither the ICF Spry Trust, nor any of the children's trusts, could be considered property or indeed even a financial resource of the parties to the marriage.

The trial judge made orders to set aside the 1998 and 2002 instruments and ordered that the assets of the ICF Spry Trust be included in the pool of assets for division between the parties.

On appeal (ultimately) to the High Court, the majority held (among other things) that the husband's legal ownership of the assets as sole trustee, combined with the wife's interest as a beneficiary of the trust, were a proper basis for the assets of the ICF Spry Trust to be treated as the property of the parties.

What does Kennon v Spry mean for trusts

Initially, *Kennon v Spry* raised concerns that the decision represented a significant widening of the Courts' power effectively to disregard the existence of a trust when considering the division of assets on a property settlement.

Over time, arguably,the practical impact of the decision has softened, due largely to the fact that the outcome of the decision appears to be strongly linked to the unique circumstances of the case. In particular, the husband'squestionable conduct – such as his mismanagement of trust assets, his threatened destruction of trust assets, his misleading representations to the Courts and attemptsto communicate directly with the judges – mighthave contributed significantly to the outcome.

Several cases since 2008 reinforce the conclusion that the impact of *Kennon v Spry* has not been as severe as initially feared. However, before exploring some of these cases, it is relevant to consider the underlying powers conferred on the Courts in relation to trusts by the Family Law Act.

Powers in the Family Law Act relating to trusts

The summary below is intended to give only a 'high level' introduction to the powers of the Family Court, in order to provide context when considering the decisions following *Kennon v Spry*.

In *Kennon v Spry*, the Court held that where:

a the husband was (at the relevant junctures) the sole trustee and appointor

b the trustee had absolute discretion to vary the terms of the trust deed and distribute income and capital to any one or more of the beneficiaries to the exclusion of any,

this was indicative that the husband was the sole controller of the trust.

The husband's control role (which meant that the husband had the discretionary power to transfer all assets of the trust to the wife), together with the wife's right of due administration as a beneficiary of the trust, was sufficient justification for the Court to determine that the assets of the ICF Spry Trust should be treated as property of the parties.

One developing issue in this regard (which is outside the scope of this chapter but warrants mention) relates to the so-called 'Jodee Rich' amendments, which in certain situations empower the Family Court to make decisions that simultaneously bind the parties to the marriage breakdown and various third parties, including creditors. This power arose from O'Ryan J's judgement in the matter of *Australian Securities and Investments Commission & Rich*[2003] FamCA 1114:

'... I have no jurisdiction to make the orders sought by ASIC *pursuant to s 90K... However, it is of concern to me that the consequence of my finding is that the Family Court has no jurisdiction to deal with an application by an unsecured or contingent creditor to set aside a financial agreement in circumstances where the interests of such a third party are or may be adversely affected by the terms of the agreement... It was therefore entered into to defeat the interests of third parties... In my view, consideration should be given to conferring jurisdiction on this Court to deal with an application by the third party whose interests may be adversely affected by the terms of a binding financial agreement to set aside the agreement. There are public policy reasons for why this should be so. Thus Part* VIIIA *should be reviewed, at least in terms of its effect on the legitimate interests of third parties, because the Family Law* Act *may be made ...an instrument of harm to a third party.'*

Section 79 Family Law Act

Section 79 applies where the Court finds that the trust assets are property of a party to the marriage,rather than a financial resource. Broadly, the four powers of the Court in relation to assets held via a trust are:

a bringing assets notionally into the matrimonial property pool
b setting aside transactions thatwould have the effect of diminishing claims under the Family Law Act
c declaring the purported trust arrangements to be a sham
d altering the ownership of a third party and making binding orders on third parties
e adjourningproperty settlement proceedings.

Determining the 'notional' pool of assets

As set out above, arguably the most important step in the making of a property settlement by the Court is the process of determining the 'pool' of assets available for distribution. Where there is clear evidence that one spouse is the true, unilateral controller of a trust holding assets accrued throughout the marriage of the parties, as well as a potential beneficiary, the Court will treat the trust assets as the property of the parties. In these situations, the assets of the trust will be added automatically to the pool.

In *Beeson & Spence*[2007] FamCA 200,it was held that, where trust assets are in fact used for the benefit of one (or both) of the parties of the marriage, the Court can 'look through' the formal legal ownership by the trustee in determining the pool of assets.

The rationale for these powers is that it would be contrary to public policy to allow a spouse with full control of assets to quarantine them, via a trust from property settlement proceedings, where the controlling spouse has the power to determine at any point to whom income and/or capital will be distributed, including to themselves.

Setting aside transactions

The Court has power under section 106B Family Law Act to set aside attempts to alter a trust relationship for the purpose of preventing the Court from adding the assets of the trust to the property pool.

In *Kennon v Spry*, the Court relied on this power to set aside the 1998 and 2002 instruments, on the basis that the amendments were undertaken for the purpose of limiting the wife's access to the assets of the trust in any subsequent property settlement. At face value, the use of the power in section 106B by the Court appeared to create a situation where the assets of a trust could be fully exposed even where:

a neither party to a marriage solely controlled the trusteeship of a trust, or

b neither party to the marriage wasa beneficiaryof the trust.

The husband in *Kennon v Spry* argued that it should be the four children's trusts (of which he was only a co-trustee, and neither he nor the wife was a beneficiary) that should be the subject of the Court proceedings.By relying on section 106B, however, the Court effectively ignored the establishment of those trusts and the purported removal of the wife as a potential beneficiary of the original trust.

Having effectively redefined the structure of the trusts, the decision in *Kennon v Spry* ultimately became a relatively 'standard' application of how the Family Court determines the notional pool of assets and should be seen as an extension of the powers as previously understood in section 106B.

Sham trusts

The Courts also have, effectively,the power to ignore a trust structure where the trust arrangement is, in fact, a sham. A trust will be treated as a sham (and its purported existence ignored) where the parties intended to create rights and obligations different from those described in the documents. Before a document is held to be a sham, it must be shown that there was the intention to mislead third parties in respect of the relevant rights and obligations in dispute.

The relatively recent decision of *Harris v Harris*[2011] FamCAFC 245 is an example of the Court considering whether a trust arrangement was in fact a sham.

In that case, the trust had been established at the instigation of the husband'sfather, prior to the husband's marriage.

The trustee of the trust was a company of which the husband and his sister and mother were directors. The husband's mother held 50% of the shares, and the husband and his sister each held 25%. At the time of the proceedings, the husband's mother was also the appointor of the trust. The husband was listed as a potential beneficiary of the trust, together with theother family members. The trust owned, amongst other assets, all the shares in a company that ran a business -initially operated by the husband and wife and, after the separation, operated only by the husband.

The wife argued that the control arrangements in place were a sham, and that the trading company (of which the husband was indisputably the managing director) was an alter ego of the husband, and on this basis the husband had sufficient control of the trust itself such that the assets of both the trust and the trading company should be regarded as being included in the property pool.

Alternatively, the wife alleged that the husband's mother was 'a puppet' of the husband, and he had indirect control of the trust through her.

The Court applied the principles set out by French CJ in *Kennon v Spry* and found that while the husband was a '*beneficiary of the trust, he did not control the trustee directly or indirectly...*' and there was no basis to notionally include the assets of the trust (including its shares in the trading company) as part of the pool of assets.

In relation to whether the trust arrangements were effectively a sham, the Court found that the wife did not advance sufficient evidence to support a finding that the husband's mother was the husband's 'puppet', through whomhe exercised de facto control of the trustee company and of the trust.

The fact that the trust had been established by the husband'sfather and that virtually every change in the management and direction of the trust could be, at least partially, referrable to the ongoing estate and the succession planning arrangements of the husband's parents, provided strong support for the conclusion that the trust was not a sham.

Altering third party ownership

Under the powers in sections 90AC and 90AE Family Law Act, the Court effectively has power to make the following orders:

a direct a third party to do a thing in relation to the property of the marriage, or alter the rights, liabilities or property interests of a third party in relation to the marriage

b restrain a person from repossession of property of a party to the marriage, or grant an injunction restraining a person from commencing legal proceedings against a party to the marriage
c direct a third party to do a thing in relation to the property of the marriage, or alter the rights, liabilities or property interests of a third party in relation to the marriage.

The practical implications of this power were demonstrated in the enforcement action following *Kennon v Spry* in the matter of *Stephens & Stephens (Enforcement)*[2009] FamCAFC 240,where it was held that:

> *'In our view, it follows that an order may be made that enables an entitlement of a party to the marriage who is an object of the trust, or ceased to be an object by reason of divorce, to be satisfied out of the assets of the trust. Put another way, an order may be made that enables a party to the marriage who is in control of the trust to satisfy his or her personal liability to the other party to the marriage who is an object of the trust from the assets of the trust.'*

Adjourn property settlement proceedings

The Court also has power in section 79(5) Family Law Act to adjourn property settlement proceedings where there is evidence that there is likely to be a significant change in the financial circumstances of the parties to the marriage and where an adjournment of the proceedings until after that change has taken place will likely do justice between the parties.

In the matter of *Grace, In Marriage of* [1998] FLC 92-792, the wife sought to have the property settlement proceedings adjourned, on the grounds that the husband was due to inherit from his father'sestate after the husband's mother had passed, as well as from a family trust.

At the time of the proceedings, the husband's mother, aged 80 years, had the use,during her lifetime,of her late husband's estate capital and income, the residue of which was due to pass to the husband (her son) and his sister in equal shares at her death. The actuarial calculation had estimated that the husband's mother mightlive for another seven years.

The husband was also named as a potential beneficiary of a family trust, which was due to vest in approximately three years from the date of the original proceedings.

The combined interest of the husband in the estate and the trust was valued at approximately $10 million.

The Court granted the wife's application for an adjournment of the proceedings until the husband's interest in the trust had vested, on the basis that there was no prejudice to the husband by adjourning the proceedings as opposed to the injustice the wife would suffer if the proceedings were to continue immediately.

Decisions following Kennon v Spry

THERE HAVE NUMEROUS reported decisions, since *Kennon v Spry*, that provide context for the exact scope of the Courts' powers under section 79 Family Law Act.

While there is little doubt about the potentially wide scope of the Courts' powers under section 79, the exercise of these powers must be supported by the underlying factual circumstances. Set out below are summaries of a few of the most relevant cases involving trusts; each explores one or more of the key themes addressed in *Kennon v Spry*. A number of the cases relates to family trusts, however the principles are relevant, by analogy, for testamentary trusts.

The cases explored are summarised under the following four headings:

- a control of trusts – the manner in which a trust is controlled
- b purpose of the trust on establishment – including the range of potential beneficiaries
- c source of trust assets
- d testamentary trusts established under an estate plan.

Control of trusts

Beeson & Spence involved a trust established by the wife during the marriage. The wife argued that the trust was established with the purpose of benefitting the children of the relationship and should not be treated as property of the marriage.

On establishment of the trust, the wife's father and her solicitor were appointed as trustees and the wife was the appointor. At a time when the husband was going through financial difficulties, the deed was varied to exclude the wife and the husband as potential beneficiaries of the trust, as well as to resign the wife as appointor. A new appointor, the wife's sister, was nominated in her place.

The husband argued that the trust was established for the benefit of the family and not just for the children.

The Court ignored the release of direct control by the wife (through her resignation as the appointor) and held that the wife still retained sufficient control of the trust to support a conclusion that the assets should be treated as property of the marriage, citing the following reasons:

'... The Deed of Variation recognised the resignation of the wife as the appointor and brought about important and fundamental changes to the Trust by appointing a new appointor and by removing the wife and the husband as beneficiaries in their own right as parents of the specified beneficiaries. Until then, the wife could have continued to lawfully control the Trust by ensuring it was administered in a manner of her choosing, including administered for her sole benefit, both as to income and capital. The recitals to the Deed of Variation suggest the wife's resignation as appointor was preceded by a request from the trustees and that, in turn, was made referable to the trustee's concern at possible insolvency and the Trust fund being placed in jeopardy. Yet whatever the thinking behind it or wherever the motivation lay, the plain fact is that nothing, including a request from the trustees, obliged the wife to relinquish control of the Trust by relinquishing the power to appoint the trustees by whose discretion it is administered. To the contrary, it was within her singular and

unquestionable power to remove the trustees and appoint another at any point. So while the recital suggests the relinquishment of the power of appointment was brought about by the trustees, it was obviously and necessarily done with the wife's co-operation and consent, which she was at no time obliged to give. Then, having relinquished control and with the new appointor installed, the Deed was altered to remove the 'parents' as beneficiaries in their own right. The steps taken via the Deed of Variation must be seen as having been taken at the wife's direction.'

In contrast, in the recent case of *Morton v Morton* [2012] FamCA 30the Court decided that, as the husband was merely a potential beneficiary and did not in fact control the trust, the trust was not his 'alter ego' on the basis that there was not sufficient control over the trust. Therefore, there was nothing to support a finding that the assets of the trust should be held to be the property of the husband.

In summary, the facts of the case were as follows:

a the couple wasmarried for approximately ten years and had no children

b at the time of the relationship breakdown the husband was a beneficiary of a discretionary trust, the Morton Trust

c the beneficiaries of the trust included: the husband, the husband's brother, his mother, any grandchildren or remote relatives and any company or trust in which the husband and his brother had an interest

d the trustee of the Morton Trust was a trustee company, J Pty Ltd, of which both the husband and his brother were equal shareholders and directors

e J Pty Ltd, in turn, owned,on behalf of the trust,a 'bucket company' known as T Pty Ltd, to which unpaid present entitlements were owed. The husband's brother was the sole director of T Pty Ltd

f the husband and his brother were the joint appointors of the Morton Trust.

The wife argued that, as the two brothers each had a 50% share of the Morton Trust and T Pty Ltd, a 50% interest should be treated as the husband's property in the property settlement. The wife claimed that the husband, in his capacity as director of J Pty Ltd, had sufficient control of the trust to support this conclusion. The husband argued that neither he nor his brother had control of J Pty Ltd as neither had a better right than the other in their standings as directors, shareholders or appointors.

The Court accepted the husband's arguments and held that the trust assets should not form part of the property pool. It was the case, as accepted by the husband, that the trust's assets were his financial resource.

The decision largely rejected a number of the wife's arguments, based on principles set out in *Kennon v Spry*.Ithighlights the importance of considering the most appropriate approach to take whenever structuring trust arrangements.

The decision in *Harris v Harris* (summarized above) provides further guidance about the relevance of actual control.In particular, it held that:

'In the present case and on the basis of the material before us the husband appears to be no more than a beneficiary of a trust. He is not the appointor of the trust nor does he hold any position in the current trustee company.

On the assumption that by the use of the word "directly", the Chief Justice was referring to the strict legal position, it therefore cannot be said that the husband "directly" controls the current trustee. Nor could it be said that he "directly" controlled the previous trustee.

On the assumption that the reference by the Chief Justice to "indirect" control of a discretionary trust by a beneficiary was a reference to a "puppet" situation, in the sense that the person with legal control of the trust is a puppet of the beneficiary, that could be the situation in the present case. In the sense, that is, of the mother (who is the appointor of the trust, and one of the three directors of the trustee company holding two shares in that company with each of the other two directors holding one share each) being the puppet of the husband. This, as was made clear by Counsel's oral submissions to us, has always been the wife's case.

The difficulty, however, for the wife on this appeal is to be able to point to any evidence which would support a finding that the husband's mother is his puppet, and that it is through her, or perhaps otherwise, that he exercises de facto control of the trustee company and of the Trust.'

Purpose of establishing the trust and range of beneficiaries

The decision of *Essex v Essex*[2009] FamCAFC 236 (**Essex v Essex**) considered the husband's interest in two family trusts, the S Trust and the N Trust. The circumstances of the case were:

a in relation to the S trust, the husband was a default beneficiary and the two children from the marriage were the capital beneficiaries

b the husband was only a general beneficiary in the N Trust, on the basis that he was the brother of the primary beneficiary
c the assets of the two trusts had largely been contributed by the husband's parents for the purpose of providing for the husband's mother's living expenses, and benefiting the husband, his brother and their bloodline
d the husband had not received distributions from either trust
e the husband's brother was held by the Court to be the controller of both trusts.

It was held in the trial Court – and endorsed on appeal -that the assets of the N trust could not be considered to be property of the spouse parties, as it was unlikely that the husband would ever receive distributions from the trust and as it was established for the primary benefit of the husband's brother's family.

In reaching his decision, the trial judge considered the control of the trusts:

'The facts in this matter are distinguishable from the majority of family law proceedings involving discretionary family trusts. Typically when discretionary trusts are involved in family law proceedings one of the parties is the appointor and, frequently, that party is also a director or major shareholder in the trustee company. In such scenarios, the requisite degree of control may be established relatively easily. This is a significant distinguishing factor from the present case, where there is little evidence that the husband has or will have control of either of the trusts. Such evidence as exists…is not persuasive.'

The trial judge initially held that the assets of the S trust were not a financial resource; however, this conclusion was overturned on appeal. The trust assets were held to be a financial resource of the husband, on the basis that:

a the trust deed terms evidenced a clear intention that the husband should benefit from the trust
b there was evidence that the husband was likely to receive distributions from the trust, following finalising of the matter.

The Full Court stated:

'...The S Trust deed evinces a clear intention that the capital of that trust be distributed on vesting, or at such earlier time as the trustee may determine, to the two children of the marriage, the grandchildren of the husband's mother. It also discloses a clear intent that the husband, as one of the three named income beneficiaries, is entitled to be considered to receive distributions of income until the vesting of the trust.'

On appeal, the Court confirmed the conclusion of the trial judge: that the trust assets could not be property of the marriage, as the husband did not have control of the trusts, nor had he contributed the assets to the trusts.

The primary questions asked of the Family Court in *Keach & Keach*[2011] FamCA 192 were whether:

a the fact that the husband was a potential beneficiary of a trust meant that its assets should be included in the pool of property
b the trust was a sham inthat the husband was in fact the true owner of the assets of the trust.

The husband's father had established a separate trust for each of his four children. The husband's trust was referred to in the judgement as 'the Junior Trust'. On establishment, the beneficiaries and residuary beneficiaries named in the Schedule of the Junior Trust were the husband and his three siblings. The father's trust was also later appointed as a discretionary beneficiary.

A corporate trustee was initially appointed for the four trusts, which at time of the marriage was Keach Nominees Pty Ltd. The father held five shares; the mother and the children (including the husband) held one share each. The father was the principal of the Junior Trust. Keach Nominees Pty Ltd retired as Trustee of the Junior Trust and was replaced by J Pty Ltd, in which the husband's brothers (but not the husband) were issued one ordinary share each.

The Court considered the following:

'...[the husband's father] established the Junior Trust, ... was the sole source of the assets, at all times... gave any necessary legal instructions to the Trust's solicitors, the accounts of the Trust were managed by an accountant under the direction of the... father... who at all times... managed and controlled the Trust, any assistance [the father] received in that regard from the husband was always under [the father's] direction... and he determined what assets the Trust would hold and acquire... attended the auction and bid for the M property... arranged the finances for the purchase by the Trust of the property... It is also noteworthy that not all allocations/distributions of the income of the Trust were made to the husband. The wife's senior counsel suggested that the evidence of this is incomplete, and it was not possible to determine the full extent of the allocations/distributions. However, I do not accept that submission. There is ample evidence to demonstrate the pattern of allocations/distributions and they certainly were not all to the husband. Indeed, it was the opposite. There

were only four allocations/distributions of income to him over a period of 23 years. I also find that the wife was under no illusion as to the ownership of the property. I consider that she was aware that the Trust owned the property from the time of its purchase...'

Accordingly, the Court held that the assets of the Junior Trust should not form part of the property pool and should be treated as a financial resource only.

Although prior to the *Kennon v Spry* decision, the case of *Webster & Webster*(1998) Fam LR 198 is relevant in this context as the husband sought to argue that the trusts in question were the 'alter ego' of the wife, and should be included in the property pool.

The facts are as follows:

a the wife was originally a beneficiary of a family trust established by the wife's (late) father. On the wife's 40th birthday, according to a letter of wishes drafted by the father, the capital of the trust was to be distributed to the wife, and any of her children, in such proportions as the trustees thought fit

b at the time ofthe distribution, two trusts were established – the P Trust and the Q trust -to receive the assets from the original trust

c the wife was the appointor of both trusts

d the wife, the wife's mother, the children and remoter issue of the wife and any spouses of the children and remoter issue were listed as income and capital beneficiaries of the P Trust

e the beneficiaries of the Q Trust were the wife, her children and remoter issue and their spouses

f the wife was the sole director of the corporate trustee of both trusts.

During the proceedings, the wife offered,to the Court and to the husband,an undertaking, (which the Court accepted) to:

'...not at any time in the future exercise, cause or permit to be exercised any position or power under the Deed dated 11 July 1996 establishing the trust known as the Q Trust which would have the effect of causing or permitting any distribution to be made to any potential beneficiary other than the said children.'

The trial judge held that establishing a trust for the protection of the children had been one of the objectives to achieve the wishes of the wife's father. To this effect, the trial judge held:

'...So while the husband's original intention appeared to accord with the wife's, by the case presented on his behalf he now seeks to shift from that by having his entitlement determined by treating the funds as owned by the wife absolutely. Of course it is the fact that the funds have been lent to ... entities, this has been done on an interest free basis and the wife, therefore, as the beneficial owner of the entities concerned has the use and benefit of the whole of the funds in her current operations. Provided that is recognised, I can see no cause to ignore the intention (initially at least shared by the husband) to benefit the children when the Trust was created and, in the light of the undertaking offered by the wife, no reason to set aside or ignore the rights and obligations created at that time by the Trust. Accordingly, it is proper, in my opinion, to view this fund not as an asset of the wife's but as a resource available to her, indeed a substantial one.

...Whether the assets of any trust are to be included in the assets available for distribution is a matter of fact to be determined taking into account various considerations. More often than not the assets of discretionary trusts are included in the net asset pool because the factual analysis suggests they ought to be. But there is no automatic assumption or presumption that they be treated this way as distinct from constituting a resource to the controlling party. Here in this case, the facts suggest that the trust was indeed specifically established for the children's benefit and protection, that was done consciously as part of the arrangements in re-settling the [original] Trust, it was a step which clearly had the support not only of the wife but also the husband at the time. That ought to be respected now.'

The Full Court upheld the earlier judgement stating that:

'... given that it was the intention of both the husband and the wife that the children would have an interest in the property or income of the trust...it was open to the trial Judge, in the somewhat unusual circumstances of this case, to conclude that the trust property should be taken into account in the proceedings as a financial resource of the wife and not as her property...In so doing, the trial Judge... was not excluding the assets held by the Trust from her consideration. We are thus not satisfied that the ground of not finding as a fact that the Q Trust was the alter ego of the wife and treating its assets as a resource rather than as assets immediately available to

the wife has been established and it is not necessary for us to determine whether, in the circumstances of this case, the trial Judge erred in accepting the undertaking given by the wife.'

The case of *Leader & Martin–Leader*[2009] FamCA 979 considered a scenario where neither party to the relationship had control of the trust assets. In this case, the wife was listed as a discretionary beneficiary of several trusts established by the wife's parents.

The wife was one of seven parties to a Family Agreement, which catalogued that the wife and her siblings were within the definition of an eligible beneficiary for a number of trusts. Under the agreement, the siblings acknowledged that '*although they qualified as beneficiaries*' under particular trusts, they agreed to direct the trustee not to consider them (or any spouse or descendant) when exercising its discretion to distribute income or capital from the relevant trust fund.

In light of this, the Court held:

'Similarly, whether the interest of the wife as a person within a class of beneficiaries is to be described as "property" or a "financial resource" is a matter which can only be determined after the full consideration of all of the relevant evidence which has been provided and appropriately tested.

On the face of the documents produced and the evidence... it appears that the ultimate control of the trusts and entities under consideration remains with the wife's parents.

Thus, the related factors of control by one party to the marriage and a potential beneficial interest of one party to the marriage which existed together in the matter of Kennon v Spry (supra) can be distinguished from this matter in which it is asserted that the wife does not have any control of any of the entities but is merely a potential beneficiary or a person falling within the class of beneficiaries. The Family Agreement between the parents and siblings is not construed to be binding upon the parents so far as their exercise of control of the trust is concerned. The Family Agreement could be construed as providing the wife with certain rights in relation to her siblings and possible other rights yet to be determined.

The decision of Kennon v Spry (supra) dealt specifically with consideration of issues relating to what was property of the husband and wife or parties to the marriage. The decision did not consider whether the entitlements of either of the parties could be described as a financial resource and thus relevant for the purposes of sections 75(2) and 79 of the Family Law Act.

In this case the wife's status as a potential beneficiary or a person who could be described as an "eligible beneficiary" is a factor which may be relevant to determining the financial resources of the wife...'

In *Edgehill v Edgehill*[2007] FamCA 1102, the wife's mother established a discretionary trust and appointed the wife as trustee and a class B beneficiary with the wife's children. The wife's two siblings were class A and C beneficiaries respectively.

Shortly after separation from the husband:

a the wife was removed as a trustee and beneficiary
b the wife's mother prepared a memorandum of wishes,part of the purpose of which, it was held, was:

'to ensure the benefit of the Trusts remaining in her bloodline for the protection of her bloodline... The effect of the memorandum of wishes is that on her death the trustees of the trust may, if the trustee acts on her wishes, re-settle the family trust into three discretionary trusts for the benefit of each of her children, grandchildren and their lineal descendants.'

The Court held that the interest was a financial resource not property and, in particular, the trial judge made the following comments:

'...There are a whole range of possibilities attaching to the ultimate benefit which the wife may receive under this trust. The recent documentation relating to the trust outlining the intention and/or request of the wife's mother in respect of how the trust should be dealt with in the future all seem to me to require the consensus of considerable number of people and having regard to human nature there would have to be, in the absence of clear evidence to the contrary, a probability that there will be a distribution under the trust some time (probably within two or three years) of the demise of the wife's mother.'

Source of trust assets

As part of the property settlement process, it is relevant to consider the contributions made by each of the parties to creating the relationship property. In this context, the Courts normally place at least some weight on the source of assets owned via a trust.

In *Simmons & Simmons*[2008] FamCA 1088 the wife argued that the husband's interest in the trust should be included in the property pool. The relevant trust was a discretionary trust, settled by the husband's father in 1979. All the members of the husband's family were potential beneficiaries.

The Court found that there was a sufficient nexus between the husband and the trust, in that he had significantly invested in the trust by personally making loans to the trust. This, in the Court's opinion, was sufficient to consider the assets of the trust to be included as the property of the parties to the marriage.

Similarly, in *Pittman v Pittman*[2010] FamCAFC 30, a trust was established with the husband listed as a general and specified beneficiary, together with his father, his mother and siblings.

The husband's father (who was the appointor and guardian of the trust on its establishment) nominated the husband's mother, the husband and his brothers, as appointors and guardians after his death. Under two later deeds, the trust fund was irrevocably appointed in favour of the nominated beneficiaries in equal shares (which included the husband).

The Court held as follows:

'... We consider that the PFT interest was property because whatever the original nature of that trust and the husband's interest in it, the various amending instruments have resulted in a situation where the husband has irrevocable entitlements not only to income, but also to a share of capital.

It is true that there is a possibility (perhaps best described as a theoretical possibility) that the husband's one quarter share of the capital might ultimately be diluted by the appointment of other beneficiaries. But he would still be entitled to some share in the capital. It is only the value of his share that might change (indeed it might increase on his mother's death).

The values of all items of property which are the subject of section 79 proceedings are likely to change between the time of such proceedings and the time when such items are eventually realised. Uncertainty of ultimate value cannot provide a reason for not categorising an item as property, and the submissions of Senior Counsel for the husband to the contrary must be rejected.

We also reject the submissions of Senior Counsel for the husband, which sought to rely on the absence of control in the husband over the trust. It is true that the husband cannot be said to have control of the trust, but that fact does not affect his irrevocable entitlements to a quarter of the income of the trust and to a share in the capital.'

While both these cases are examples of howtrust assets were treated as property of the marriage, as opposed to merely a financial resource, they also demonstrate the needfor a significant level of control and nexus to support this conclusion.

Testamentary trusts established under an estate plan

Although the decision of *Ward v Ward*[2004] FMCAfam 193 was prior to *Kennon v Spry*, it is important because it was one of the first to consider the application of the Courts' powers to a testamentary trust established under a will.

Before their divorce,the parties had a 30-year marriage, which had produced two children. The Court was required to adjudicate a number of issues, one of which was how to treat the husband's interest in a testamentary trust.

The will of the husband's mother established a testamentary trust and it was admitted that the dominant purpose in establishing the trust was to protect the husband's inheritance. The trustees of the testamentary trust were the husband's two sisters. The range of beneficiaries included the husband and his two children, but not the wife.

An earlier draft of the mother's will had included the husband as a co-trustee and executor. Shortly before her death, when she became aware of the husband's marriage difficulties,she had amended it to exclude the husband from these roles.

At the time of the proceedings, by the Court's acknowledgement, there was no evidence of any expectations or distributions under the testamentary trust to any of the beneficiaries.

The Court found the circumstances as being similar to those in the matter of *Bonnici & Bonnici*, discussed above.

The Court acknowledged that it was probable that the husband would receive the whole entitlement of the testamentary trust at some point. Despite this, it was held that the interest of the testamentary trust could not be considered property of the husband. Accordingly, the Court found that the interest was merely a financial resource of the husband and that the wife had contributed very little to creating it.

The more recent decision of *Lovine v Connor*[2011] FamCA 432considered the assets in two testamentary trusts (which were administered as one testamentary trust) established in the husband's father's will approximately nineyears before the separation of the parties.

The Court found the following facts:

a the beneficiaries of the testamentary trusts included the husband, his two sisters and their respective children
b the husband's sisters had each effectively received their one third interest in the assets of the testamentary trusts
c the remaining assets of the testamentary trusts represented the one third share of the estate held for the husband, and it was the ultimate intention of the husband to distribute the testamentary trust assets to himself and/or his children
d the husband was the only real controller of the testamentary trusts and althoughthe will appointed the husband's sisters as

joint trustees with him, they played no active role in the control of the testamentary trust.

The husband argued that the assets of the testamentary trusts should only be classified as a financial resource. However, the trial judge determined (and it was later upheld on appeal) that due to the husband's control over the assets and the real likelihood that he would ultimately receive the benefit of the assets, the assets of the testamentary trusts should be treated as property of the marriage.

Practical recommendations

IT IS CLEAR, from *Kennon v Spry* and subsequent decisions, that the Family Court has extremely broad powers beyond ordinary trustlaw principles when dealing with trust assets in a property settlement.

As with any Court decision, the outcome in relation to a particular trust will often depend on the exact facts and circumstances. It can be argued, however, that recent decisions indicate that each of the following characteristics tend to lead to theconclusion that trust assets should be considered to be property of the parties to the relationship:

a where both spouses are able to benefit, and historically have benefited fully, from the income and capital of a trust
b where a spouse is the controller of a trust -for example, as the sole trustee orappointor, or through a shareholding or directorship of a corporate trustee
c where the property of a trust has been contributed by the parties to the relationship, or through the efforts of a party to the relationship
d where the property of the trust was acquired during the relationship.

In the light of these broad principles, it is also possible to draw some practical conclusions from recent court decisions, as outlined below. Many of these principles are particularly relevant when structuring trusts to facilitate the intergenerational transfer of wealth – during a person's lifetime and under anestate plan.

Obviously, any steps taken to structure trustsshould be considered and implemented as part of a comprehensive review, and ideally not immediately prior to thebreakdown of a relationship. As outlined above, *Kennon v Spry* is a clear example of the Courts' ability to use the powers in section 106B to unwind unilateral changes to a trust once there is evidence that a relationship is becoming strained.

Structuring testamentary trusts

When establishing testamentary trusts as part of an estate plan, it is relevant to consider whether a separate testamentary trust should be established for each child, or if all children should effectively share their inheritance jointly via a single testamentary trust.

There are many issues that should be taken into account when deciding whether to use a single, multiple or 'hybrid' testamentary trust. As with many estate planning issues, there is no 'correct' approach, as relevant factors will vary,depending on the situation.

Broadly, a single testamentary trust will most likely be preferable if:

a some or all of the children are minors. The primary focus in this situation should be on the surviving spouse; it is therefore not ideal to have wealth held across multiple testamentary trusts where the surviving spouse will likely be in control for many years
b the will makerenvisages that the children should act as custodians of the wealth for future generations
c the main objective of establishing the testamentary trust is asset protection
d the nature of the assets (such as a real property) would render a split-ownership structure unnecessarilycomplicated.

In contrast, a multiple testamentary trust – that is, a testamentary trust established for the benefit of each child – mightbe more appropriate, despite offering less security in the case ofa relationship breakdown, if:

a the children live in different geographical locations
b the relationship between the children is poor – an important consideration, as the joint control of wealth might further deepen existing rifts between family members

c there are significantdifferences betweenthe risk profiles of each child's investment outlook
d the underlying nature of the trust assets makes a single testamentary trust impractical – for example, where particular assets areearmarked for the sole control of a particular beneficiary
e there is a desire to implement different control mechanisms for each child (in this context one child mightbe the sole controller of their trust, whereas another child mightrequire a co-trustee or be wholly excluded from being a trustee).

The 'hybrid'testamentary trust approachcombines elements of a single testamentary trustwith those of multiple testamentary trusts. Generally, in this approach, a set percentage of the estate (or certain assets) is distributedto a 'head testamentary trust', the control of which is shared between the various family members and any independent trustees. This head trust will include all lineal descendants as potential beneficiaries.

Sub-testamentary trusts are then created for each child (and their respective spouses and lineal descendants) and separate assets are gifted to each. The children will usually control,and independently regulate succession of,their own sub-testamentary trust.

The above approaches will be considered in more detail in Chapter 5.

Letters of wishes

Another factor that Family Courts have considered relevant, particularly in recent times, is the use of a letter of wishes, which is often prepared by a will maker (in the case of a testamentary trust) or by a significant contributor to a trust.

A letter of wishes is typically a non-binding document that gives guidance to the trustees as to how they should ideally exercise their discretionary powers to administer a trust's assets.

In both *Breakspear & Ackland*[2008] EWHC 220 (Ch)(**Breakspear & Ackland**) and *Read & Chang*[2010] FamCA 876 (**Read &**

Chang), the Courts ordered disclosure of the relevant letters of wishes. The predicament specifically considered by Brigg J in *Breakspear & Ackland* was that the disclosure of such confidential documents would cause them to lose favour with those wishing to establishtrusts, arguably resulting in both less favourable and less helpful information for trustees.

On the other hand, a letter of wishes is often crucial to determining the manner in which the trustees are likely to exercise their powers. Therefore, withholding disclosure may reduce the practical extent to which trustees can be held accountable and courts canmake informed decisions about how to factor a trust's assets into a property settlement.

In *Read & Chang*, Cohen J acknowledged the decision in *White & Tulloch v White*,which found that the key criterionin determiningwhetherdisclosure is appropriate is whether the evidence is, or mightbe, relevant to the just and equitable process under section 79 Family Law Act. In particular, the likely relevance will depend upon the nature of the claims being put forward and the overall facts of a particular case, or as the Court held:

> '...*Although trustees should primarily regard themselves as having a duty to withhold disclosure of a confidential memorandum of wishes ... the Trustees and Court ought determine whether countervailing circumstances, including the likely relevance of the wishes of the person at whose request the trust was created, warrants disclosure.*'

In the light of these cases, if trustees are concerned about protecting the confidentiality of letters of wishes, they should consider advancing no reasons at all for the decision to withhold the letter as, if they do advance such reasons, the Court is entitled (upon application by a beneficiary), to enquire as to the reasonableness of the trustee's decision.

Read & Chang,in particular, demonstrates this point. In that case,the trustees admitted to being influenced by the memorandum of wishes in making past income distributions to the wife from the relevant trust. This admission gave credence to the husband's argument that the letter would better inform the Court about future distributions, and the Court, therefore, examined the relevant document before making its decision.

Range of beneficiaries

As noted above, when structuring trusts, careful consideration should always be given to the range of potential beneficiaries and, in particular, whether spouses should be included. Generallyspeaking, it is difficult for the Family Court to draw a sufficient nexus between a trust and the parties to a relationship where the relevant spouse has never been a beneficiary of the trust.

In the case of *Essex v Essex*, themere *possibility* of receiving trust distributions was confirmed as being sufficient to support a finding that the trust was a financial resource. In particular, the Court held:

> '...*The husband was a named income beneficiary of the S Trust. The husband at no time sought to remove himself as a beneficiary, and the husband's brother's attempt to do so had no relevant purpose (other than to attempt to put the trust's assets beyond the reach of the Court).Significantly, as the sole director of the corporate trustee of the S Trust the husband's brother had control of that trust and was only obliged to consider the husband as one of the three income beneficiaries entitled to the income of the trust. However, the husband's brother conceded that, but for a disqualifying factor (the property proceedings) the husband should have the benefit of assets in the trusts. This in our view required the*

trial Judge to find that the S Trust was a financial resource of the husband.

Distributions

It is common for parents to use trust assets to helpchildren make personal investments -for example, in the purchase of a family home. Rather than by simply distributing or gifting assets to the relevant child, parents can achievesignificant asset protection by arranging to havefunds loaned by the trust, with appropriate security taken over the assets acquired by the child.

Similarly, trust assets can often be drawn inadvertently into the property pool where there are unpaid present entitlements or credit loan accounts owing to a party to the relationship breakdown. In cases where the trust owes a debt to a spouse, that amount will be included as an asset of the spouse without the need to consider the issues outlined above in relation to the trust.

Binding financial agreements (BFA)

Wherethere is a desire for greatercertainty that trust assets will not be exposed in a property settlement, consideration should be given to implementing a BFA. It can be a useful tool to limit the application of the Family Courts' powers in relation to trust assets. Further commentaryon these agreements, however,isoutside the scope of this chapter.

Chapter 4

PROTECTIVE TRUSTS, OTHER SPECIAL TYPES OF TESTAMENTARY TRUSTS AND PRACTICAL CONSIDERATIONS FOR TESTAMENTARY TRUSTS

Introduction

TRUSTS THAT FALL within the framework of charitable trusts include trusts established for religious, educational or scientific purposes.

Trusts for charitable purposes can be created *inter vivos* or on death, via a will. Apart from providing a mechanism to achieve the philanthropic objectives of the founder, there can also be taxation benefits if the trust meets the requirements of the ATO.

Having considered the various asset protection benefits of testamentary trusts, this chapter will consider varioustypes of trust structures available for protective purposes as well as other special types of testamentary trusts.

The chapter will also explore some practical considerations in relation to testamentary trusts, including how they can be varied.

Achieving charitable purposes

A SIGNIFICANT FOCUS IS placed on ensuring that charitable trusts can meet the requirements of the ATO in order to obtain certain endorsements, exemptions and concessions. Importantly, however, just because a trust meets the requirements of the ATO, it is not automatically a valid charitable trust under trust law.

Creating a failed charitable trust, by will,might result in the intended assets of the failed trust being distributed to the residuary beneficiaries named in the will or to the beneficiaries entitled on intestacy. Therefore, when drafting a testamentary charitable trust, it is important to consider the possibility of certain parties attacking the validity of the trust in order to take a greater share of the estate.

Elements of a valid charitable trust

The three certainties

Like any other express trust, a charitable trust must satisfy the requirements of certainty of intention and subject.In contrast to other forms of express trusts, a charitable trust does not need to satisfy the beneficiary principle(which requires that a trust must exist for identifiable beneficiaries). Instead, a charitable trust must exist for a charitable purpose that benefits the general community, or a sufficient section of the community.

Vesting of the trust

Charitable trusts are not subject to the rule against indestructible trusts;this means that the trust can exist indefinitely. However, the rule against perpetuities still applies, meaning that the trustee's interest must vest within the perpetuity period – *Re Goode (dec'd)* [1960] VR 117. This is especially important to consider when drafting conditional gifts, as outlined below.

The rule against perpetuities is subject to the provisions in the various state-based property related legislation (**Property Law Act**) which creates a 'wait and see' rule.

The 'wait and see' rule provides that where the disposition fails under general law for breaching the rule against perpetuities, it is not void immediately; it is possible to wait and see whether the interest actually vests within the perpetuity period.

Preamble to Statute of Charitable Uses 1601

The preamble to the *Elizabethan Statute of Charitable Uses 1601* is the accepted starting point in defining the legal meaning of charity. The preamble identifies the following purposes as charitable:

a relief of poverty
b care of aged persons and the sick
c care of soldiers and mariners
d advancement of education through universities and schools
e repair of bridges, havens, ports, churches and highways
f care of orphan
g maintenance of prisons
h marriage of poor maids
i support for young tradesmen and persons decayed
j relief or redemption of prisoners or captives
k relief for poor persons, concerning the payment of taxes.

Four heads of charity

The leading case of the *Commissioner for Special Purposes of Income Tax v Pemsel* [1981] AC 531 identified four heads of charity namely:

a relief of the poor
b advancement of education
c advancement of religion
d other purposes beneficial to the community.

Gifts for pets

Trusts for individual pets are not considered charitable, because:

a there is no beneficiary with legal identity
b the gift to the pet does not satisfy the beneficiary principle
c there is no overriding charitable purpose.

However, the courts can accept types of trusts for non-charitable purposes, including those for the benefit of a will maker's animals. The fiduciary obligations of the trustee of these trusts are generally not enforceable, so if the trustee elects not to comply with the terms of the trust, the subject of the trust reverts to the residuary estate.

A purported gift to a pet potentially leaves the estate exposed in two ways:

a the risk of a trustee 'making a deal' with the residuary beneficiaries – that is, the trustee chooses not to carry out the trust in consideration for a payment by the residuary beneficiaries
b even if the trustee wants to carry out the trust, the pet has no competing claim under the legislation in each state allowing challenges against wills. This meansthat if the will maker fails to provide adequately for the proper maintenance and support of a child, spouse or dependant, the gift to the pet will likely be removed, thereby creating a greater pool of funds from which to provide for the aggrieved family member.

For example, in *Goodchild v James* (1994) 13 WAR 229 the will maker's will included a gift of $50,000 to his dog, Blacky. The estate was worth $130,000 and no provision was made for one of the will maker's sons. The Court removed the gift to Blacky, having regard to the competing moral claims of the other beneficiaries and the son for whom no provision had been made.

Gifts to a particular pet or pets are treated differently from gifts to animal shelters or for the prevention of cruelty to animals, which are generally considered as being charitable in nature. Often, therefore, a better way to secure the future of a pet is to make a gift to the RSP-CA and express the wish that the RSPCA care for the relevant animal.

Compendious gifts

At general law, trusts with mixed charitable and non-charitable purposes are void unless it is possible to sever or apportion the charitable and non-charitable purposes or if the purposes can be read cumulatively.

The phrase 'charitable purpose' is presumed to be exclusively charitable. However, the term 'philanthropic' has been defined to mean 'a purpose which indicates good will to mankind in general'. Philanthropic has been held to be too broad to come within the legal concept of 'charity'.

This potentially means that a gift that reads as follows would fail at law on the basis that it is not exclusively charitable:

'I give ten thousand dollars to the RSPCA for its charitable and philanthropic purposes.'

Where a gift would otherwise fail at law, a court may apply legislative created powers if the trust significantly indicates a charitable intention.

These powers generally provide as follows:

'(1) *No trust shall be held to be invalid by reason that some non-charitable and invalid as well as some charitable purpose or purposes is or are or could be deemed to be included in any of the purposes to or for which an application of the trust property or funds or any part thereof is by such trust directed or allowed.*

(2) *Any such trust shall be construed and given effect in the same manner in all respects as if no application of the trust property or funds or of any part thereof to or for any such non-charitable and invalid purpose had*

been or should be deemed to have been so directed or allowed.

(3) *This section shall not apply to any trust declared before, or to the will of any testator dying before, the commencement of this Act.'*

When drafting charitable gifts, it is essential to use words that have already been interpreted to be exclusively charitable – that is,to avoid words such as 'benevolent' and 'philanthropic'.

Conditional gifts

In *Re Dyer*[1935] VLR 273, a gift to help create a fund to establish and maintain an orchestra was expressed to be contingent on a fund sufficient for that purpose being subscribed. It was impossible to say with any degree of certainty whether such an orchestra would exist in the future, let alone within any definite period of time, or be established at all. As the condition precedent to the gift might never have been fulfilled, it was held to infringe the perpetuity rule and consequently the gift reverted to the settlor.

Public benefit

There is a rebuttable presumption that trusts for the relief of poverty, advancement of religion and advancement of education are of benefit.

Such benefit must be for the general community or for a sufficient section of the community:

'Section of the public' has been defined as 'any group which any member of the public could belong to if he or she chose to live in a particular area or adhere to a particular faith.'

A trust established for the benefit of individuals dependent on their relationship to a particular individual or employer will not satisfy the requisite public benefit element unless the trust is for the relief of poverty.

For instance, in *Oppenheim v Tobacco Securities Trust Ltd* [1951] AC 196, there was a gift 'for the education of children of employees of a certain company'. The House of Lords held that limiting the benefit to the children of employees of a certain company denied the gift the requisite public element even though the total number of employees of the group of companies exceeded 110,000.

Gifts to schools

Gifts to schools are valid, even if the school charges fees, provided the fees are not so high as to exclude all but the extremely wealthy and the school does not have a 'profit making' purpose.

'Profit making' is defined as follows:

'Institutes are prima facie charitable unless they exist for a private profit. The reference to private profit does not refer to the payment of wages or allowances to employees of or other service providers to the charity but to the distribution of the profit and or capital of the institution to private institutions (or non-charitable entities), whether during the operation of the institution or on its winding up.'

The constitution of the school and any related foundation should be examined to ensure that any profit made by the school or the foundation is to be applied in the furtherance of the basic educational aims of those entities and not distributed to private individuals.

The concepts of 'profit making' and the 'exclusion of all but the extremely wealthy' should also be considered when drafting charitable trusts to benefit hospitals and aged care facilities.

Administration and enforcement of charitable trusts

The rule against testamentary delegation dictates that will makers cannot, by will, delegate to others a complete discretion as to how to dispose of their property. However, this rule does not apply to gifts of a charitable nature.

Where there is a general charitable intention, as opposed to a specific charitable intention, a court can save a charitable trust that would otherwise fail by applying a general scheme or a *cypres* scheme (explained below).

Particular charitable intention

A particular charitable intention is where the settlor clearly intends to benefit the stated object exclusively and no other and shows an intention that the gift should fail if it cannot be put into effect as stated. For example, in *Re Good's Will Trusts* (1950) 2 All ER 653, a particular charitable intention was found in a bequest to establish a rest home for the aged.

The gift failed from the outset as there were insufficient funds to achieve the stated objective and there was held not to be a general charitable intention, by reason of the will maker's specification of detailed plans in relation to the home, which included proposed rules of admission, proposed management powers and instructions as to its layout.

There is a long line of authority to support that where there is a bequest to a specific institution that no longer exists there is a specific charitable intention.

General charitable intention

A general charitable intention is a direction that is not essential to the trust. For example, in *Attorney General (NSW) v Perpetual Trustee (Milly Milly Case)* (1940) 63 CLR 209, a farm was left on trust to be used as a training farm for orphaned boys. The farm was in poor condition and needed a lot of maintenance work. It was decided that the farm was unsuitable for the specified purpose.

The Court found that the use of the farm itself was not an indispensable part of the trust. There was a general charitable intention and a *cy pres* scheme was applied to provide farm training in another way.

So that a charitable gift can be saved, it should expressly state that a 'general charitable intention applies'.

Generalscheme

The court will apply a general scheme where the original charitable purpose can be achieved and where the donor has exhibited a general charitable intention but has provided inadequate instructions or has made provisions that require the continuing supervision of the trust.

Cy pres scheme

The court will apply a *cy pres* scheme where the stated purpose cannot be achieved and the court will alter that purpose to some other purpose as 'near as possible' to the donor's original intention.

State-based legislation dictates the specific cases where *cy pres* schemes may be ordered. In particular, there is:

a the requirement of general charitable intention where there is failure of the original purpose

b a duty on the trustee to apply for a *cy pres* scheme where the case permits.

Summary

In summary, the main issues to consider when drafting charitable trusts are as follows:

a it should be statedspecifically, in the establishing document, that the donor has a general charitable intention so that there is no question as to the ability of the court to apply a scheme

b conditional gifts should not be used, so as to avoid breaching the rule against perpetuities

c terminology outside of the word 'charitable' should not be used, so as to avoid creating compendious or mixed purpose gifts;

d it is important to identify correctly any institution that is intended to benefit – preferably by ABN or some other unique identifier -and especially where gifts are made to organisations which might havebranches in various geographic locations

e where commercially appropriate, the opinion of counsel or a specialist lawyer should be considered

f in the event of failure of the charitable trust, the document should includeprovisions for redirecting the subject of the trust -for example:

'...if this gift fails for any reason, I give the subject of the gift to (a), (b) and (c).'; and

---

g an *inter vivos* charitable trust mightbest suit the circumstances and should be considered. The value of an estate will be reduced by the creation of an *inter vivos* trust, potentially deterring parties who would otherwise have attempted to obtain provision from the deceased estate.

Accommodating special disability

Special Disability Trusts (SDTs)

SDTs provide an opportunity for benefits that are effectively ignored for the purposes of calculating pension entitlements to be directed to a qualifying beneficiary.

Historically, trust assets were largely ignored for Centrelink purposes. However, Centrelink rules in respect of trusts and their effect on pension entitlements changed on 1 January 2002. The changes meant that, subject to the terms of the trust, Centrelink was able to attribute all capital and income of a trust to the beneficiary.

Despite these changes, if the beneficiary qualifies for a SDT, assets up to $609,500 as at 1 July 2013 will be ignored for pension calculation purposes. The SDT must meet special requirements, which can be found in 'Special Disability Trusts', a publication by the Department of Families, Community Services & Indigenous Affairs.

What is a SDT?

The Federal Government originally introduced SDTs into social security legislation in 2006; significant changes have been made, due to the lack of interest in utilising the structure historically.

The primary purpose of SDTs is to encourage private provision of accommodation and care for people with a severe disability or medical condition, through concessional taxation benefits.

Any individual can establish a SDT, via an *inter vivos* deed or pursuant to a person's will.

A SDT must meet the following requirements:

a it can have only one beneficiary
b the beneficiary must meet all 'eligibility' criteria set out in the relevant legislation

c the primary purpose must be to provide for the accommodation and care needs of the beneficiary
d it must have at least one independent trustee
e it must comply with the prescribed investment restrictions
f it must prepare annual financial statements and carry out independent audits when required.

The Department of Human Services will assess whether a trust is a SDT. This exercise involves determining whether the prospective beneficiary meets the definition of 'severe disability' under section 1209M *Social Security Act 1991*(Cth) (**Social Security Act**). The Department of Human Services suggests that the assessment of whether the intended beneficiary will qualify should be made before the preparation of the trust deed.

Each principal beneficiary can have only one SDT and each SDT can have only one principal beneficiary. The principal beneficiary can, however, be a potential beneficiary of other trusts in addition to the SDT.

SDTs are not allowed to receive compensation payments that are paid to, or on behalf of, or held in trust for the principal beneficiary.

On the death of the principal beneficiary, the trust ceases to be a SDT and assets are distributed as stipulated in the trust deed.

Who can be the principal beneficiary?

To be eligible as a principal beneficiary, the person with the disability must meet the definition of 'severe disability', which is:

a a person who has reached 16 years of age
  (i) whose level of impairment would qualify the person for Disability Support Pension or who is already receiving a Department of Veterans' Affairs (DVA) Invalidity Service Pension or DVA Invalidity Income Support Supplement
  (ii) who has a disability that would, if the person had a sole carer, qualify the carer for Carer Payment or Carer Allowance

(iii) who is living in an institution, hostel or group home in which care is provided for people with disabilities and for which funding is provided under an agreement between the Commonwealth, the states and the territories
(iv) who has a disability as a result of which he or she is not working and/or who has no likelihood of working for more than seven hours per week at or above the relevant minimum wage

b a child under 16 years of age
(i) who is a profoundly disabled child, as defined in section 197(1) of the Social Security Actand who was a principal beneficiary immediately before 1 July 2009
(ii) who is a person with a severe disability or a severe medical condition
(iii) where another person, the carer, has been given a qualifying rating of intense under the Disability Care Load Assessment (Child) Determination for caring for that child
(iv) where a treating health professional has certified in writing that, because of the disability or condition:
(I) the child will need personal care for six months or more
(I) the child care is required to be provided by a specified number of persons
(v) where the carer has certified in writing that the principal beneficiary will require the same care, or an increased level of care, to be provided to him/her in the future.

Where the above criteria are satisfied, all of the SDT's

a assessable assets are attributed to the beneficiary
b income is exempt from the means test for the purposes of calculating the beneficiary's income support payments, as long as all of the trust income is used only for the benefit of the beneficiary and related administrative purposes.

Who can access the gifting concessions for a SDT?

The intended beneficiary's immediate family members who are at, or over, service pension age and are receiving a pension – for example, age pension or carer payment – may be eligible for the gifting concession.

Where there is more than one contributor to the SDT, the combined concession first applies to those eligible family members who are receiving a pension after age or service pension age.

An immediate family member includes:

a natural parents
b legal guardians
c adoptive parents
d step parents
e grandparents
f siblings.

What amount of money can a person contribute to the SDT?

Contributions or gifts of assets to any value can be made to a SDT at any time. However, the rate of a contributor's pension and/or allowance might be affected if the contribution is more than the allowable concessional amount and/or if the contributor does not meet the required eligibility criteria.

Gifts can affect a pension or allowance because they directly or indirectly reduce the assets available for personal use. Contributors must inform the Department of Human Services of any gifts or transfers within 14 days of when they have occurred.

Any gift or number of gifts whose total value is greater than the allowable concessional amount will be assessed under normal pension gifting rules.

A gifting concession applies to gifts up to $609,500 per SDT.

This concessional amount can only be used once. For example, if an eligible contributor who receives a pension gifts $400,000 and receives the gifting concession, then another eligible contributor who receives a pension and gifts $300,000, can only receive $209,500 as a gifting concession.

The additional $90,500 will be assessed under the normal gifting rules.

What can the SDT funds be used for?

Income and capital of the SDT can be used to meet the reasonable care and accommodation needs of the beneficiary.

Some examples of reasonable care needs are: specialised food, mobility aids, sleeping aids, modifications to vehicles, transport requirements, daily care fees charged by an approved provider in relation to the beneficiary's care, and accommodation in a residential care service.

Some examples of reasonable accommodation needs are: modification to the beneficiary's place of residence, payment to fund the purchase of the beneficiary's place of residence, rental payments for the beneficiary's place of residence, and payment of accommodation bond.

From 1 January 2011, a SDT can undertake a level of discretionary spending that is not directly related to the care and accommodation needs of the beneficiary, provided that the expense complies with legislative requirements. The current level of discretionary spending is set at $10,750 (indexed annually on 1 July). Some examples of such 'discretionary' expenditure are: toiletries, recreation and leisure activities, computer equipment and household cleaning services.

Protective trusts

THE CONCEPT OF a protective trust stems from a strategy, established in the United Kingdom, to protect property from an individual's creditors and from that individual'sunwise disposal of the property.

Broadly, the strategy has two stages:

a Stage 1: A trust with a fixed income distribution to the principal beneficiary, until a 'termination event' occurs. The termination event canbe, for instance, the bankruptcy or death of the principal beneficiary. This first stage essentially establishes an equitable determinable life interest for the principal beneficiary
b Stage 2: On the 'termination event', the fixed income distribution ends and the trustee instead holds the income to distribute, at its discretion, among a range of objects -normally the principal beneficiary (if living) and members of their family. No beneficiary has a vested interest, merely an expectancy and a right to be considered.

Ultimately, protective trusts guarantee an income stream to the principal beneficiary but, if a 'termination event' occurs, the income stream ceases and a discretionary trust is established.

The standard provisions of a protective trust have been recorded in trust legislation. However, a protective trust may also be established by a trust instrument, to suit the circumstances of a particular family or beneficiary.

Example legislation – protective trusts

Definition	'Protective trusts' means the trusts specified in this legislation,or any like trusts;'the principal beneficiary' has the same meaning as in this legislation;'discretionary interest' means an interest arising under the trust specified in this legislation,or any like trust.
Legislation	(1) Where any income, including an annuity or other periodical income payment, is directed to be held on protective trusts for the benefit of any person (the principal beneficiary) for the period of the principal beneficiary's life or for any lesserperiod, then, during that period (the trust period) the income shall, without prejudice to any prior interest, be held on the following trusts, namely: (a) upon trust for the principal beneficiary during the trust period or until the principal beneficiary, whether before or after the termination of any prior interest, does or attempts to do or suffers any act or thing, or until any event happens, other than an advance under any statutory or express power, whereby if the said income were payable during the trust period to the principal beneficiary absolutely during that period, the principal beneficiary would be deprived of the right to receive the same or any part thereof, in any of which cases, as well as on the termination of the trust period, whichever first happens, this trust of the said income shall fail or determine;

	(b) if the trust to which paragraph (a) refers, fails or determines during the subsistence of the trust period, then, during the residue of that period, upon trust for the application thereof for the maintenance, education (including past maintenance or education), advancement or benefit, of all of any 1 or more exclusively of the other or others of the following persons (that is to say) - (i) the principal beneficiary and his or her wife or husband (if any), and his or her issue (if any); (ii) if there is no wife or husband or issue of the principal beneficiary in existence, the principal beneficiary and the persons who would, if the principal beneficiary were actually dead, be entitled to the trust property or the income thereof or to the annuity fund (if any), or arrears of the annuity, as the case may be, as the trustee in the trustee's absolute discretion, without being liable to account for the exercise of such discretion, thinks fit. (2) Nothing in this section operates to validate any trust which would, if contained in the instrument creating the trust, be liable to be set aside.

Incentive trusts

In the United States, incentive trusts, which are designed to encourage or discourage the behaviour of beneficiaries, are commonly used in estate planning, particularly in relation to financially irresponsible beneficiaries. For instance, there may be a requirement to complete a university degree before a capital distribution can be made, or the trust might pay a dollar of income for every dollar the beneficiary earns.

There is no reason why a similar concept cannot be applied in Australia; however,there is a risk that such a trust (or at least the limitations imposed by the trust) could be declared void for reasons such as:

a public policy
b trustees being prohibited from fettering their discretion.

As is the case with a protective trust, the limitations imposed on income and capital distributions by incentive trusts hinder the trustee in accommodating changes in circumstances as they arise and in managing distributions to minimise income tax.

Superannuation death benefits trusts

A SUPERANNUATION DEATH BENEFITS trust – also known as superannuation proceeds trust (**SPT**) – is a trust that is established solely to receive superannuation proceeds on the death of a fund member. A SPT can be established by a will or by deed after the death of an individual.

The *Income Tax Assessment Act 1997* (Cth) (**ITAA 1997**) provides that a superannuation death benefit, paid to a death benefit dependant as a lump sum, is not assessable income.

A death benefit dependant (defined under section 302195 ITAA 1997) is a:

a spouse or former spouse of the deceased
b child, aged below 18, of the deceased
c person with whom the deceased had an 'interdependency relationship', as defined by section 302-200 ITAA 1997
d person financially dependent on the deceased just before they died.

Where there are death benefit dependants, under a deceased estate,who are potential recipients of superannuation benefits, it is often appropriate to allow for a separate SPT under the will in addition to any testamentary trust, so that a tax free distribution of the superannuation proceeds can be achieved via a protected structure. Other estate assets can be distributed to a testamentary trust that has beneficiaries who are not 'death benefit dependants'.

A death benefit received by a legal personal representative (**LPR**) is treated as income to which no beneficiary is presently entitled. The LPR is, therefore, liable for any tax liabilities under section 99 ITAA 1936.

Where the superannuation proceeds are paid to a SPT, the LPR is taxed in accordance with how the person or persons intended to benefit from the estate would be taxed were they to have received the payments directly. That is, the ATO will generally adopt a 'look through' approach as if the death benefit had been paid directly to the recipient.

To ensure that any receipt of superannuation proceeds is tax free, the LPR should ensure that, at least on receipt of the superannuation proceeds by the SPT, the only capital beneficiaries of the SPT are those who meet the definition of 'death benefit dependant' under section 302-195 ITAA 1997.

In practical terms, this means that where there is more than one death benefit dependant, the terms of the SPT should provide that they receive the trust capital in specified shares on vesting.

In particular, ATO Interpretative Decision (**ID**) 2001/751 (which has since been withdrawn on the basis that its view has been subsumed into section 302-10 ITAA 1997) confirms that it appears to be the clear intention of the legislation that the fact that a payment is made to a trustee, rather than directly to the dependant, should not obscure the fact that the payment is ultimately for the benefit of the dependant. In the facts considered in ATO ID 2001/751, the death benefit dependant was the sole beneficiary of the trust and, therefore, absolutely entitled to the income and capital of the trust.

The requirement that death benefit dependants receive the capital on the ending of the trust is also driven by the requirements of section 102AG(2) ITAA 1936, which sets out the basis on which trust property must be regulated when the trust ends, in order to access the excepted trust income provisions.

There is limited guidance about whether the ATO will require all the income beneficiaries of a SPT to be death benefit dependants. The conservative position would be to limit the income beneficiaries of the SPT to death benefit dependantsonly. In particular, the guidance available in relation to whether tax will be payable on receipt of the superannuation proceeds under section 302-10 ITAA 1997 indicates that the income and capital beneficiaries should be limited to death benefit dependants.

It is arguable,however, based on the ATO's comments in Taxation Ruling 98/4, that a SPT can include a broad range of discretionary income beneficiaries. While Taxation Ruling 98/4 sets out the ATO's view in relation to child maintenance trusts, established to access the concessional taxation rates for minors under section 102AG ITAA 1936, it can be argued that the comments apply to all such trusts (including SPTs).

Taxation Ruling 98/4 also confirms that the trust deed (or will) may contain mechanisms to prevent the rule in *Saunders v Vautier* (1841) EWHC Ch J82 from applying – that is, that the beneficiaries can agree to wind up and distribute the assets of a trust among themselves where they are absolutely entitled to the trust property. One example in this regard is to include additional discretionary income beneficiaries, so that a child cannot call for the distribution of trust property upon attaining 18 years.

In practical terms, it appears that the ATO only tests the range of potential beneficiaries of the SPT at the date at which the superannuation proceeds are received by the SPT (for example, see private ruling authorisation number 1011741138466). Therefore, even to take the conservative approach – that is,initially to limit the range of potential income beneficiaries to ensure tax free receipt of insurance proceeds under section 302-10 ITAA 1997, following receipt of the superannuation proceeds – it may be possible for the range of beneficiaries to be expanded to include non death benefit dependants.

For completeness, as superannuation proceeds do not automatically form part of the estate of the deceased member, it may be necessary to ensure that appropriate nominations are made by the member to direct that the superannuation death benefits are paid to the LPR for distribution under the will, and if appropriate, to any SPT established.

Establishing a SPT after death

A form of SPT can also be established after the death of the member, and can be useful where there are substantial superannuation assets within a deceased estate and where there is a death benefit dependant, but where the will maker had not incorporated testamentary trusts into the will.

When relying on this approach, difficulties can arise as, in many cases, superannuation fund trustees might not have discretion to pay proceeds to a SPT under their trust deed. Furthermore, many trustees appear to adopt an interpretation of the superannuation laws that prohibits any such payment. Often there is no clear pathway to allow the trustee of a superannuation fund to distribute to a SPT unless the SPT has been established under the deceased's will.

Child maintenance trusts

Overview

Child maintenance trusts are specifically provided for in section 102AG ITAA 1936. As with many of the other forms of trusts dealt with in this chapter (such as superannuation proceeds trusts and special disability trusts), the main advantage of child maintenance trusts is the ability for income of the trust to be treated as excepted trust income.

A child maintenance trust, like most trusts, must be established by deed but, in contrast to many other trusts, cannot be created under a will. There are also other requirements that must be met before the income of the trust is treated as excepted trust income, including:

a the children named as the 'primary beneficiaries' of the trust must be younger than 18 at the time the trust is established
b income must be derived by the investment of property transferred to the trustee of the trust for the benefit of the beneficiary/beneficiaries, as a result of a 'family breakdown'. The definition of a 'family breakdown' is relatively wide; however, reference should always be made on a case-by-case basis to the definition set out in ITAA 1936
c there is no set time frame in which a child maintenance trust must be established following the family breakdown
d the children for whose benefitthe trust is established must ultimately receive all of the capital from the trust in equal shares
e the potential income beneficiaries of the trust may include persons other than children of the relationship subject to the family breakdown.

Where income is held to be excepted trust income it effectively means that any infant children who are beneficiaries of the trust and are entitled to income of the trust will each have access to the normal adult rates of tax – that is, the first $24,000 (approximately) worth of income tax free, with the balance at normal adult rates.

Non arm's length arrangements

The income of a child maintenance trust which results from non arm's length transactions must, however, be of equal value to that which would have been derived on an arm's length basis in order to be considered excepted trust income for the purposes of Division 6AA ITAA 1936.

Essentially this means that if, for instance, a loan made by a child maintenance trust to a parent was not at arm's length, but at a more favourable interest rate compared with prevailing market rates, then the income derived by the trust will have been less than if the transaction was at arm's length. In this type of situation, section 102AG(3) ITAA 1936 reduces the amount that may be treated as excepted trust income.

The arm's length requirement is set out in detail in section 102AG(3) ITAA 1936. In particular, this section provides that if any two or more parties to:

a the derivation of the excepted trust income mentioned in subsection (2); or
b any act or transaction directly or indirectly connected with the derivation of that excepted trust income,

were not dealing with each other at arm's length in relation to the derivation of income, or in relation to the act or transaction, the excepted trust income (if any) is only so much of that income as would have been derived if they had been dealing with each other at arm's length in relation to the derivation, or in relation to the act or transaction.

One alternative tax effective strategy, often used in establishing a child maintenance trust, is to contribute depreciating assets such as plant, equipment and motor vehicles to the trust. These assets can be leased, either to a related individual or a business entity for value.

Provided the lease repayments are on an arm's length basis, then the income will be able to be distributed to infant children as excepted trust income.

Taxation Ruling 98/4 sets out in detail the Commissioner for Taxation's position in relation to child maintenance trusts.

Estate proceeds trusts

ESTATE PROCEEDS TRUST can be either an 'estate proceeds' trust (where the proceeds were originally part of a deceased estate), or a 'non-estate proceeds' trust (where the proceeds originate from an asset which does not form part of the deceased estate). Two common examples of non-estate proceeds are superannuation entitlements and life insurance.

An 'estate proceeds' trust is a trust established by a deed after the death of the deceased. It is most commonly used to obtain advantageous tax treatment for income allocated to minor beneficiaries – that is, excepted trust income, as explained above.

Generally, an estate proceeds trust is more restrictive than an ordinary testamentary trust established pursuant to the terms of a will. An 'estate proceeds' trust differs from an ordinary testamentary trust on account of the following features (section 102AG ITAA 1936):

a minor beneficiaries (persons under 18 years of age on establishment of the trust) must be the ultimate capital beneficiaries of the trust, meaning the assets of the trust must ultimately vest in them
b the transfer of estate assets to the trust must occur within three calendar years of the date of death of the deceased
c the income that may pass tax concessionally must not exceed that which would have been derived from the entitlements that the minor beneficiaries would have received if the deceased had not left a valid will (that is, if the deceased had died intestate).

The main advantage of an estate proceeds trust, other than providing a level of asset protection (particularly for wastrel beneficiaries), is the concessional tax treatment of income distributed from the trust and the ability to split income according to the financial circumstances and needs of the deceased's children.

The income distributed from the trust may be used to pay for the children's education, living and other expenses; any income received by a minor will be taxed at the normal adult rate, rather than the penal rate that normally applies to income distributions to infant children.

As noted above, this means that, assuming the children are not earning other income, they will be eligible for the $24,000 (approximately) tax free threshold for income received by each child per financial year. Any additional income will be taxed at the ordinary adult marginal rates.

There are numerous technical issues that must always be reviewed before establishing an estate proceeds trust, including:

a the concessional rates of tax are very unlikely to be available to the grandchildren of the deceased

b as noted above, while assets in excess of what the will maker's children might have received on an intestacy can be contributed to the estate proceeds trust, only the income generated by that portion of the capital which the will maker's children would have received on an intestacy will be entitled to the concessional rates of taxation

c any assets that do not form part of the will maker's estate (such as assets owned as joint tenants with a spouse, or insurance policies that are owned by the surviving spouse) will not be able to be contributed to the estate proceeds trust.

Conclusion

THE RANGE OF bespoke trust structures is almost limitless. It isimportant, therefore, to have the exact purpose and outcome of the trust in mind prior to its establishment. Apart from adverse tax and duty consequences that can arise from an ill-considered structure, the risk of a complete failure of an intended trust is significant.

Adding testamentary trusts to existing wills after the will maker loses capacity

An individual can only make a valid will whilst having the mental capacity to do so.

If an individual loses lawful capacity, legislation in each state provides that the court may, upon application by an appropriate person, make a will for, or alter or revoke the will of, an individual who lacks capacity.

Re Matsis

In *Re Matsis: Charalambous v Charalambous & Ors* [2012] QSC 349, the Supreme Court of Queensland considered an application for a court authorised codicil (that is, an amendment to an existing will) for Mr Matsis, a 90 year old man who lacked capacity.

Mr Matsis' surviving family members were his adopted daughter and her three sons. Under Mr Matsis' existing will, he gifted a house to one of those grandsons and split the residue of his estate between the three grandsons in equal shares.

The applicant, being one of the grandsons, submitted that a codicil be made to amend the will to give the residuary estate to three testamentary trusts for each of the grandsons, rather than passing to them outright.

The following matters were considered relevant by the Court:

a Mr Matsis' estate was worth more than $13 million
b Mr Matsis' daughter was not in need of provision from his will
c two of the grandsons were engaged in businesses and, as a result, were potentially exposed to liability (although there was no evidence of any current exposure to liability)

d it would be advantageous from an estate planning perspective to have the substantial gifts to the beneficiaries held upon testamentary trusts
e in the terms of the draft codicil presented to the Court, the estate would pass to the same persons and in the same proportions
f Mr Matsis' long standing solicitor was of the view that, had he explained the benefits of testamentary trusts to him, Mr Matsis would have made a will including them, due to his entrepreneurial skills and his desire for his grandsons also to possess those skills
g Mr Matsis had lost lawful capacity due to severe dementia and it was not likely that he would regain capacity prior to his death.

The Court ultimately approved the terms of the draft codicil presented to it as being a codicil that Mr Matsis mighthave made, had he the capacity. The legislation in Queensland does not require that the codicil be one that the incapacitated individual would make, but rather it requires simply that it be a document the individual might make, if he or she had the requisite capacity to do so.

The Court was also satisfied that the test set out in *In Re D(J)* [1982] Ch 237 (**In Re D(J)**) had been met. However, it should be noted that the approach of *In Re D(J)* has been departed from in the United Kingdom, as a result of the decision in *Re P* [2009] EW HC 163 (Ch). That case sets out a number of factors, at pages 243-244, which should be taken into account, including:

'...it is to be assumed that the [incapacitated individual] is having a brief lucid interval at the time when the will is made.

...

...during the lucid interval the [incapacitated individual] has a full knowledge of the past, and a full realisation that

as soon as the will is executed he or she will relapse into the actual mental state that previously existed, with the prognosis as it actually is.

...

...I think that during the hypothetical lucid interval the [incapacitated individual] is to be envisaged as being advised by competent solicitors.'

Arguably, the important factors,here,that assisted the Court in making its decision included:

a evidence showed that the will maker regarded the will that was in place before he lost capacity as an 'interim' document;
b the only person who could have brought a challenge against the estate was the will maker's daughter, who indicated in the proceedings that she was independently wealthy and had no intention of challenging the estate
c the ultimate beneficiaries of the estate (those bringing the application) were the will maker's grandsons. While each of them potentially had asset protection risks, they were aware of any potential litigation
d the change to the existing will did not alter any of the provisions in relation to, for example, executorship or any specific gifts
e while the grandsons lost direct entitlement by the inclusion of the testamentary trusts, they were still ultimately the likely potential beneficiaries via the trust structures
f the Court accepted evidence that the will maker himself may well have implemented testamentary trust provisions, had he not lost capacity.

Further decisions

The above decision should be compared with *Hausfeld v Hausfeld & Anor* [2012] NSWSC 989 (**Hausfeld**), which involved an unsuccessful application for a court authorised will in the Supreme Court of New South Wales.

Mr Hausfeld was a widower and had three children. Mr Hausfeld's previous will gave his estate to the three children equally.

One of those children, Gregory, made the application for the court authorised will, seeking that his one-third share be gifted to his wife instead of to him as he was involved in litigious proceedings and, if those proceedings were successful, he could be found to be liable for the payment of substantial damages and likely be required to declare bankruptcy.

Gregory submitted that his father would not want his share of the estate to vest in the trustee in bankruptcy and therefore it should be gifted to his wife on the understanding that she make provision for him, if needed.

The Court ultimately dismissed the application for public policy reasons. White J stated that:

> *'In my view it is not appropriate, nor might it become appropriate, for the Court to authorise an alteration to Colin Hausfeld's will in order to defeat his son's creditors.'*

It could be argued that this decision questions the ability of the Court to make a will for an incapacitated person, for estate planning and asset protection reasons.

However, *Hausfeld* was distinguished by the Supreme Court of Queensland in a subsequent decision, *Doughan v Straguszi & Ors* [2013] QSC 295. In that case, Ms Straguszi owned a farm and the court authorised will proposed to establish testamentary trusts naming various family members to hold the family farm. The motivation for the establishment of the testamentary trusts was that one of her sons was involved in a business in receivership.

Henry J distinguished *Hausfeld* on the basis that the proposed court authorised will did not attempt to gift the son's share to another person to defeat creditors, but, rather, to ensure that the family farm was preserved for future generations.

The above highlights:

a the test for court authorised wills differs state to state – for example, the test set out in the Queensland legislation is broader than it is in New South Wales, which is highlighted by comparing section 24(d) *Succession Act 1981* (Qld) with section 22(b) *Succession Act 2006* (NSW);

b each case must be determined on its particular facts

c the concept of using applications for court authorised wills for estate planning and asset protection reasons is a developing area of law.

Varying testamentary trusts – can the will allow for it?

MANY MODERN TESTAMENTARY trust will precedents include a power to vary.

The power is commonly drafted to be quite broad, but may be limited so as not to:

a infringe the law of perpetuities; nor
b affect the entitlement of a beneficiary, which has been set aside prior to the variation.

Without an express power, a testamentary trust can only be varied by a court.

Delegation of testamentary power

When including a power to vary in a testamentary trust will, it is important to bear in mind the rule against delegation of testamentary power.

Power to vary should be exercised cautiously

A power to vary the terms of a testamentary trust included in a will should be exercised cautiously.

In summary, it is generally accepted that the circumstances in which a power to vary can be exercised are:

a any limitations or conditions contained in the power to vary must be followed precisely
b even when following the exact provisions of the variation power, the trustee must also exercise the power with their fiduciary

duties in mind – that is, to act in the best interest of the beneficiaries of the trust as a whole

c the likely intentions of the person establishing the trust (in the case of a testamentary trust, this is obviously the will maker) must be considered and any variation should align with the original objectives of the settlor

d the variation should not fundamentally change the terms of the trust such that the 'substratum' is affected. One example of this concept is where a particular clause is mentioned in the variation power as being unable to be amended; however, the variation power itself has no such prohibition. Some trust advisers would argue that, if the variation power itself is first amended to remove the prohibition on amending a particular clause, and then a subsequent variation amends the clause that has had the restriction removed, this 2-step process may amount to a variation to the core trust itself (that is, the sub stratum) and therefore would be void.

Varying the trust through other means – court orders

Power to seek court orders

Generally, all beneficiaries of a trust need to be adult and of sound mind and in agreement,with one another and with the trustee (and appointor if necessary), as to any court-approved variations to the terms of a private trust. Australia wide, the courts have the power to vary the terms of trusts. This extends to testamentary trusts.

In determining whether it is appropriate to vary a trust, the court will take into account the intention of the person establishing the trust, as it appears from the terms of the trust deed and other evidence available.

The court will not necessarily authorise the insertion of a blanket power of variation into a trust deed. Instead, it prefers to authorise specific variations. This point was highlighted in *Re, in the matter of the Alan Synman Family Trust* [2013] VSC 364 (**Re Alan Synman Family Trust**).

In*Re Alan Synman Family Trust*, the trustee of a family trust applied to the Supreme Court of Victoria for a general power of variation to be inserted into the deed pursuant to section 63A *Trustee Act1958* (Vic)to give effect to the intention to benefit Mr Synman's family and to correct some drafting errors. Court approval was required because some of the beneficiaries were grandchildren under the age of 18 years.

It was necessary for the trustee to satisfy the Court that the proposed power to vary would benefit the grandchildren. Otherwise, the Court could not approve the variation. Some of the proposed variations (for which, the trustee submitted, the power of variation would be used) were beneficial for the grandchildren – for example, adding the grandchildren to a particular class of beneficiaries; however, the Court was not satisfied that all possible variations would be.

In dismissing the application, Ginnane J explained at paragraph 26:

> *'In this, and in most applications under s 63A, the appropriate path is for a trustee to seek the Court's approval of an arrangement to vary specific provisions of the Trust Deed, rather than seeking approval of an arrangement giving the trustee a general power of variation. By the former path, the Court can, in most circumstances, best assess whether the carrying out of the arrangement would be for the benefit of persons who have an interest under the trust and who are incapable of giving their assent. It is far more difficult to reach that conclusion when the Court does not have the detail of all the variations that the trustee will make, once given the general power of variation.'*

The comments in this case may be particularly relevant to testamentary trusts because these trusts are often drafted as LDTs.

Vesting a testamentary trust when beneficiaries are sui juris at the vesting date

A TRUST MUST HAVE a lifespan that complies with the law of perpetuities.

In all states and territories except South Australia and the Northern Territory, legislation has overridden the common law to provide that the perpetuity period of a trust is no more than 80 years from the date of creation of the trust.

In South Australia, a trust is not required to have a perpetuity period.

In the Northern Territory, the perpetuity period of a trust can be either a life in being plus 21 years or 80 years from the creation of the trust, whichever is specified in the trust instrument.

The terms of a testamentary trust should set out the circumstances in which the trust shall vest and who shall receive the remaining assets of the trust on the vesting date.

Testamentary trusts often specify that the vesting date is 80 years from the creation of the trust (that is, the death of the will maker) or such date earlier as the trustee or appointor may decide.

As most testamentary trusts are discretionary trusts, the trustee will often have the discretion to distribute the assets on the vesting day to any one or more of the beneficiaries in any proportions the trustee considers appropriate. If the trustee fails to or does not make a decision, default provisions may determine the basis on which the assets must be distributed on the vesting day.

Practically speaking, the default provisions should rarely need to be relied upon, as a prudent trustee would be mindful of the vesting date of the trust and would exercise the discretion to distribute the trust property on or before that date.

The considerations of a trustee when the vesting date is approaching are summarised in the following questions:

a should the trust property be sold with the net proceeds of sale then distributed to the beneficiaries?
b should assets be transferred to beneficiaries as they are – that is, as an '*in specie*' distribution?
c what are the revenue consequences (both tax and stamp duty) of each distribution alternative?
d have the provisions of the trust deed been reviewed and complied with?
e have all loan accounts and unpaid present entitlements with beneficiaries been satisfied?
f which beneficiaries will receive the distributions?
g have all legal, accounting, tax and statutory requirements of both the trustee and the trust itself been complied with?
h how will the records of the trust be stored following vesting?

Practical considerations

A trustee has a duty to keep accurate records. Therefore, it is important that the decision to vest a testamentary trust is appropriately recorded, in the form of trustee minutes resolving to do so pursuant to the terms of the trust.

The trustee is also responsible for ensuring that the assets are actually distributed to the beneficiaries and should do so in a timely way, whether that be by forwarding a cheque to the beneficiaries if their entitlement is cash, or by arranging documentation to give effect to the *in specie* transfer of assets such as real property or shares, or by a combination of cash and *in specie* distributions. The trustee should also obtain a receipt from the beneficiaries to confirm they have received their entitlement.

Chapter 5

COMPLEX FORMS OF TESTAMENTARY TRUSTS: MASTER TRUST AND MULTIPLE TRUSTS

Introduction

WHILE THE MARKETPLACE has largely accepted the benefits of using testamentary trusts to pass wealth efficiently, the range of options that atestamentary trustcan provide and the advantages that variations from a 'standard'testamentary trust present can easily be overlooked. It is more often the case that the decision to utilise testamentary trusts is the beginning, rather than the end of the estate structuring process.

Having considered the various types of protective and special testamentary trusts, this chapter considers:

a testamentary trusts generally and common variations and issues with single testamentary trust structures
b the utilisation of multiple testamentary trusts, and when they should be used
c the increasingly common variations, sometimes referred to as 'master' testamentary trusts, including commentary about the alternative meanings, common purposes and taxation treatment of these structures.

Review of testamentary trusts

AT ITS SIMPLEST, atestamentary trust is a trust that is formed on the death of the will maker. The terms of the trust are set out in the deceased's will. For this reason, advisers often refer to testamentary trusts as 'will trusts'.

While this term is a relatively useful plain English label, it is applied in defiance of the reality that all wills effectively contain terms of a trust, with the executors as trustees and the inheritors the beneficiaries.

Testamentary trusts usually refer to a more extended and operative trust arrangement than the bare trust created by any will. Most testamentary trusts are testamentary trusts operating not unlike 'normal' *inter vivos* discretionary trusts, complete with classes of potential beneficiaries, extensive powers and unfettered discretions as to distributions of income and capital.

Common variations and issues with simple testamentary trust structures

Multiple testamentary trusts

It is not uncommon for each intended beneficiary to become the trustee of their 'own' testamentary trust (**Figure 5.1**).

This means that, instead of receiving one-third control of an entire estate, the person is in sole control of a testamentary trust that holds one-third of the estate, with the ability to distribute the income or capital of the trust to themselves or family members as the beneficiary sees fit.

This is often desirable because it is easy to delineate what the beneficiary is receiving.

Figure 5.1

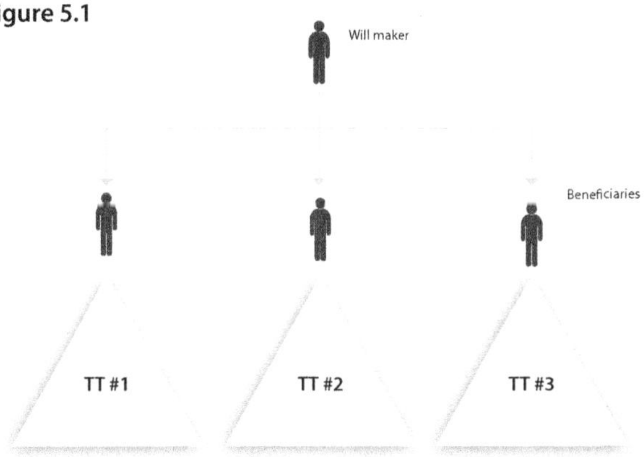

Another common benefit is that any remaining assets of a testamentary trust (that is, not distributed out of the testamentary trust during the lifetime of the beneficiary) will normally pass into the control ofthe children of that beneficiary on their death. This flexibility can:

a. prevent the potential for family provision application in most states, except potentially New South Wales
b. have the effect of passing the benefits of the testamentary trust structure 'down the line' of descendants of the original patriarch and matriarch.

Multigenerational issues for single testamentary trusts

The basic transparency of a 'one testamentary trust per main beneficiary' approach can be complicated by the reality of most nuclear families, particularly those with baby boomer patriarchs and matriarchs, because of the nature of trusts.

If one spouse dies leaving the estate to the other (as is most often the case), one testamentary trust is often formed (**Survivor's Testamentary Trust**). This scenario is complicated, significantly, where the surviving spouse outlives the other for an extended period, due to the likelihood of remarriage and (sometimes) further children. The main, conflicting, issues that arise in this regard are:

a. the surviving spouse cannot 'write a will' for the assets held in the Survivor's Testamentary Trust as they are not personal assets. This issue can be managed to some extent by careful passing of trust control mechanisms
b. often the surviving spouse can distribute the assets out of the Survivor's Testamentary Trust at any time, which means the assets may be consumed or bequeathed according to the spouse's will
c. the surviving spouse could gift their assets (via their will) to the originally created Survivor's Testamentary Trust.

On the death of the surviving spouse (which, as noted, may occur either in quick succession or alternatively many years after the death of the other), the single testamentary trust model creates logistical and administrative issues where the couple have more than one child. In particular, the structure of the roles of trustee, appointor and beneficiary will be relevant.

The complications of a single testamentary trust are often exacerbated with each additional child. The issues are often wider than just being 'locked in' or having differing ideas as to investing and distributing trust assets. For example:

a there may be more children than the number of allowed trustees (in most states the limit is four)
b if one of the children of the second generation passes (or has passed) away, leaving children of their own, it will be difficult and cumbersome to administer the testamentary trust in the interests of all potential beneficiaries (including the deceased child's direct descendants). The discretionary nature of testamentary trusts can become a double-edged blade in these circumstances.

'Cougars' and 'cradle-snatchers'

One of the highest profile risks of a multigenerational estate plan is remarriage,after the death of one partner to a relationship. Many commentators have remarked, and many families discovered first hand, the practical issues that result from the remarriage and subsequent death of the surviving spouse.

Where the survivor of the original relationship updates their estate plan to provide for their new spouse and then predeceases them (statistically likely where the new spouse is significantly younger than the first spouse!) then assets from the first marriage may flow in part or whole to the new spouse, who may feel little or no obligation to provide in their will for the children of the first marriage.

Single testamentary trusts only partially solve this problem if control of the spouse's testamentary trust, created on the death of the first spouse, is to be passed to the children of the first marriage.

However, if instead the surviving spouse has the requisite control, they can of course distribute the capital of the testamentary trust to themselves. This can effectively mean that the result is often the same as if the original couple had only simple (as opposed to testamentary trust) wills (**Figure 5.2**).

Figure 5.2

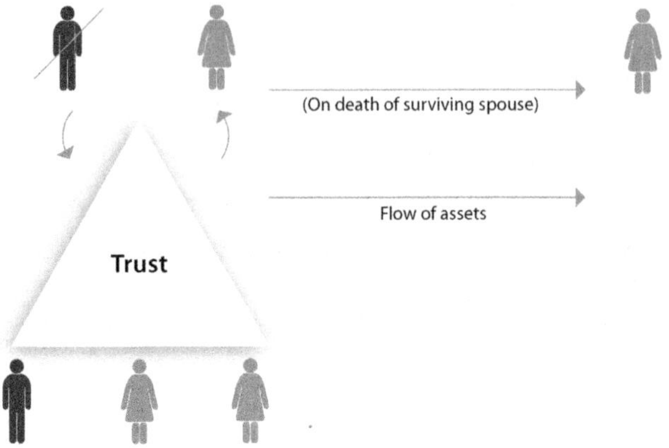

'Hybrid' solutions

It is not always necessary to abandon completely the single testamentary trust structure in favour of multiple testamentary trusts. Often a single testamentary trust can provide the required platform in one or more of the following ways:

a the classes of beneficiaries can exclude certain members of the family
b inclusion of mandatory succession of control provisions
c inclusionof restrictions or prohibitions on the ability to distribute capital of the trust
d mandating the passing of control, including the trusteeship and powers to remove and appoint trustees.

Simple examples of the approaches summarised above can include appointing a joint trustee (often independent) to act with and 'balance' an otherwise spendthrift beneficiary, or delaying the receipt of powers of appointorship until a beneficiary reaches a certain age.

In other circumstances, implementing a form of master trust will be appropriate.

Optional testamentary trusts

Some wills are structured to give the executor, with the consent of the primary beneficiary of the relevant testamentary trust, discretion to ignore or bypass the testamentary trust. This type of structure is sometimes known as an 'optional testamentary trust'.

Circumstances where it might be appropriate for an executor and beneficiary to elect to ignore a testamentary trust and pass assets directly to a beneficiary include:

a where the value of the assets are not significant enough to justify the administrative burden of the testamentary trust and the taxation and asset protection advantages are not required
b to ensure there is access to the main residence exemptions for Capital Gains Tax (**CGT**) or land tax, where the asset passing to the testamentary trust will be the beneficiary's residential home
c there has been a change to the legislation, which means the testamentary trust is no longer appropriate.

However, there is a risk under the 'optional testamentary trust' structure that a beneficiary may elect to bypass the testamentary trust without obtaining appropriate advice about the taxation and asset protection benefits or considering the intentions of the will maker.

Where a will has been drafted so that the testamentary trust is not optional, there will generally be power for the trustee to vest the testamentary trust if it is determined that the structure is no longer appropriate.

Where the trustee is given this power, the approach still gives flexibility to wind up a testamentary trust, whilst reducing the risk of assets passing to a beneficiary absolutely without obtaining appropriate advice. Generally, there are also CGT and stamp duty exemptions available when assets are transferred to the beneficiary on the winding up of a testamentary trust.

What are 'master trusts'

Master trusts are commonly used to identify either of the following two situations:

a a 'cascading' testamentary trust that seamlessly passes the capital from a single testamentary trust in the first generation to multiple testamentary trusts in the second generation (**Cascading Testamentary Trust – Figure 5.3**). This typically resolves many of the above issues with single testamentary trusts in the second generation and third generations without (necessarily) sacrificing flexibility

b a single holding trust to preserve the family wealth over the course of generations, with a 'custodial' mindset, rather than one of ownership (**Traditional Master Trust – Figure 5.4**). Access to the capital (and occasionally the income) is carefully managed for the advancement of family members without giving away or dividing the 'family jewels'.

The Traditional Master Trust structure is increasingly common within the high and ultra high net worth (**HNW** and **UHNW**) sector.

Each of the above concepts is dealt with in turn below.

Cascading testamentary trusts

A Cascading Testamentary Trust arrangement is one development of the single testamentary trust structure that provides further degrees of flexibility in trust structures.

Typically, a Cascading Testamentary Trust is one where:

a one 'head trust' holds the estate of one deceased spouse on trust for the surviving spouse and direct descendants
b the surviving spouse has full control of income and, with the consent of one or more beneficiaries, the timing of the distribution of capital
c there is a proviso that capital may only be distributed, without the requisite consent, into one or more further testamentary trusts established under the same will for the benefit of the next tier of beneficiaries. This might occur automatically on the death of the surviving spouse or earlier at the surviving spouse's option
d normally, the second tier of testamentary trusts is controlled by the children of the original couple, with their lineal descendants as further potential beneficiaries.

Figure 5.3

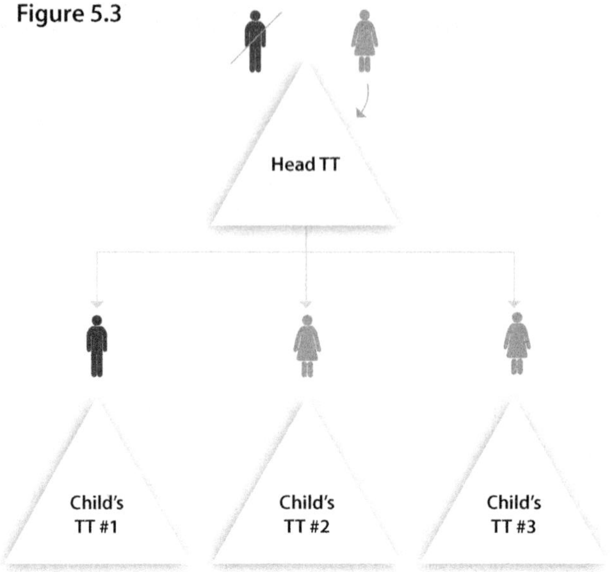

The above approach effectively preserves the capital of the estate and facilitates a further division into manageable discrete trusts, to be controlled by the next generation of surviving children. The result can provide a seamless transfer through at least one further generation while maintaining a much more flexible 'life interest' style outcome for the surviving spouse.

As a result Cascading Testamentary Trusts, when drafted correctly, can also address many of the multi-generational issues above.

Variations on cascading testamentary trusts

It is possible to continue to create further 'tiers' of Cascading Testamentary Trusts into the subsequent generations. However, the combined term of all layers of the testamentary trusts will likely be subject to the limitation imposed by the law against perpetuities (in all states, other than South Australia). This will mean that the testamentary trust structure must end within 80 years from the death of the first will maker.

Another reason for the limitation of Cascading Testamentary Trusts to one tier is the desirability of not 'locking up' the assets and removing control over the distribution of capital for extended periods of time. Other than ensuring that the benefit of their estate flows to the next generation and possibly to a third, most will makers will be ambivalent as to how wealth is managed further down the line by their descendants.

There is also increasing uncertainty about the concessional tax and stamp duty treatments that Cascading Testamentary Trusts have enjoyed to date, as discussed further below. For this reason, as well as the ongoing focus on trusts by the ATO and other revenue authorities, it might be advisable to limit regulated distributions of capital in the short to medium term.

Tax treatment

There has been some uncertainty regarding the taxation treatment of the subsequent transfer of a CGT asset from the trustees of a Cascading Testamentary Trust to the second tier testamentary trust.

In most circumstances, where a trust distributes its capital, CGT event E7 will happen under section 104-85 ITAA 1997.

However, proponents of a Cascading Testamentary Trust arrangement generally seek to rely on the exception contained in Division 128 ITAA 1997. This rule allows any capital gain or capital loss made on a post-CGT asset to be disregarded if, when a person dies, an asset they owned passes:

a to their LPR or to a beneficiary; or
b from their LPR to a beneficiary.

Taxation Ruling 2006/14 states that a 'trust to which Division 128' ITAA 1997 applies means:

'... a deceased estate to the extent that it is a trust over an asset originally owned by a deceased individual and which may pass to the beneficiary in accordance with section 128-20 (that is, under the will, by intestacy and so on).'

'In the context of CGT events E5, E6 and E7 this means that the exception applies if subsection 128-15(3) applies to relieve any capital gain or capital loss that arises (or would apply in that way if there were a capital gain or capital loss) when an asset passes from the deceased's legal personal representative to a beneficiary in their estate.'

In 2003 the ATO released Practice Statement LA 2003/12which states that its purpose is to inform staff that the Commissioner will not depart from the long-standing administrative practice of treating the trustee of a testamentary trust in the same way that a 'legal personal representative' is treated for the purposes of Division 128 ITAA 1997.

As explained in more detail in Chapter 6, this is generally accepted to mean that there is an exemption from CGT covering the 'transfer' from the LPR to the trustee of the testamentary trust in the first instance as well as the subsequent transfer to an eventual beneficiary of the estate.

Furthermore, it would appear that the exemption applies in the context of Cascading Testamentary Trusts for the subsequent transfer to the second tier testamentary trust. However, as noted above, the appropriateness of moving forward the Cascading Testamentary Trust structure may be in doubt.

CGT

Should the exemption summarised above not apply, then CGT will be triggered in the same way as for deceased estates normally, that is:

a the difference between the will maker's original cost base and the market value of the asset at the date of the distribution to the second tier testamentary trust; or
b where the asset was a pre-CGT asset in the hands of the deceased, the increase in value since the death of the deceased to the date of distribution.

Given the significant potential disadvantage for the cascading structure if the taxation treatment is ever revised, thought should be given, in each instance, as to what the beneficiaries' options are after the death of the first spouse. For example, the surviving spouse's testamentary trust might specifically include an ability to distribute capital to the beneficiaries directly prior to the vesting date.

Part IVA

There is a significant potential benefit from a taxation perspective in the Cascading Testamentary Trust approach (as with those of any testamentary trust) in that there is effectively a '3 stage' transfer of estate assets before a CGT event would occur, which may be effectively delayed until the asset is transferred to the hands of a beneficiary, up to 80 years after the death of the original will maker.

As is the case with standard testamentary trusts, given the Cascading Testamentary Trust is predominantly driven by estate and succession planning considerations,it is unlikely that Part IVA ITAA 1936 should be applied.

Duty treatment

As is the case with almost every transaction that may be subject to stamp duty, the position in each state is different.

Particularly in the area of Cascading Testamentary Trusts, it is critical to consider the specificfactual circumstances and then overlay both the terms of the relevant stamp duty legislation and the practical application of that legislation by the relevant revenue authority.

As a general rule, any distribution under a will is exempt from stamp duty in each state.

From a stamp duty perspective, the issues in relation to Cascading Testamentary Trustsare in many respects similar to the CGT position. In other words, while the initial transfer into a Cascading Testamentary Trust seems to satisfy clearly the exemption provisions in each state, any subsequent transfers out of a Cascading Testamentary Trust could be subject to a duty impost.

On the face of the legislation in most states and territories, there seems to be a reasonably arguable position that subsequent transfers out of a Cascading Testamentary Trust (either into a sub-trust or to an ultimate beneficiary) should be exempt from stamp duty.

In at least two states, however, the interpretation applied by the relevant stamp duty authorities is that no exemption applies. In one state, this interpretation represents a change in what has otherwise been a long-standing approach.

Other transactions involving Cascading Testamentary Trusts (perhaps the most relevant being the movement of funds by way of loan and security arrangements), also differ from state to state. There are, in some instances, proposed changes to the rules but although there have been publicly announced timetables for implementing the changes, there have also been deferrals of the proposed starting date.

Ultimately, when a client is considering a Cascading Testamentary Trust. it is important to flag the potential stamp duty costs and to emphasise the overriding need to seek specific advice at the relevant time.

Traditional master trusts

Traditional Master Trusts, sometimes referred to as 'head' or 'dynastic' trusts, are generally distinguished from a single testamentary trust structure that selectively makes the distributions available over time, with limited access to capital. The defining feature of Traditional Master Trustsis that they provide each generation with a more custodial role, preserving and increasing the corpus of the original legacy for the benefit of descendants.

Traditional Master Trusts and derivations have proven to be a popular method for the holding and preservation of wealth in HNW and UHNW families. Increasingly, families in these segments are seeking to put in place more structured 'custodial' arrangements to maximise the impact and preservation of family wealth over a greater reach of future generations.

Due to the focus on the role of 'trustee of the family wealth' rather than on ownership and consumption of wealth in a particular generation, the structure must be carefully considered and tailored to achieve the wishes of the first will maker. Typically there is only one testamentary trust with more prescriptive governance, succession and administrative provisions than a standard testamentary trust.

Generally, capital is only made available to family members on a secured basis, often via interposed family trusts. Other provisions might allow limited access to funds at specific milestones or to assist with specific personal investments, including education or the purchase of homes.

Often, these provisions will represent the 'greatest good for the greatest number' approach by leveraging the application of wealth to points of need or merit amongst the future family members of the budding 'dynasty'.

Figure 5.4

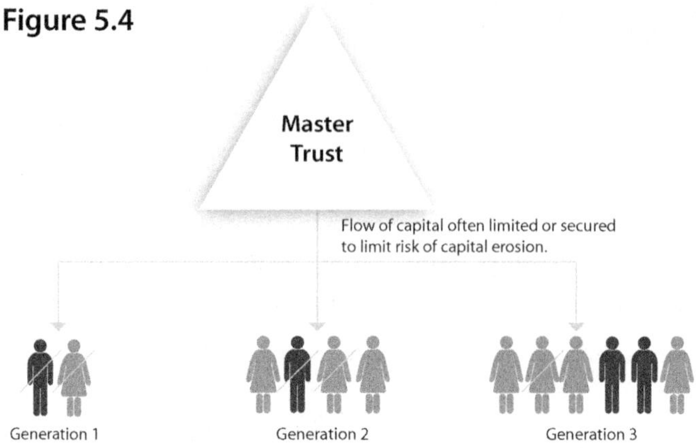

CGT and stamp duty

Unlike Cascading Testamentary Trusts, the majority of the trust estate is held in the same trust until distribution. As there is no transfer of capital assets out of the Traditional Master Trust, the duty questions that relate to Cascading Testamentary Trusts (as outlined above) simply do not arise.

Law against perpetuities

As touched on earlier in this book, in all multigenerational structures the effective 'deadline' for ultimate wealth distribution presented by the law against perpetuities is a relevant consideration.

In Traditional Master Trusts, where the corpus of the trust is not expected to be expended or distributed for an extended period of time, the potential CGT triggered on final vesting of the trust is a significant issue. A further question is how to effect the desired 'dynastic', long-term operation of the trust when it has what is effectively an 80-year deadline in most Australian jurisdictions.

South Australia is unique at the present time in that the law against perpetuities has essentially been abolished. This potentially removes these issues for Traditional Master Trusts where the operative law is that of South Australia.

While the scope of this book does not provide an in depth examination of the various issues surrounding operative law (some broad comments are set out in Chapter 6), it is important to consider this issue in the specific context of any Traditional Master Trust arrangement. For many clients, at least some thought should be given as to whether it is possible to establish a master trust regulated by South Australian law.

Distribution of benefit and voting rights

Traditional Master Trusts represent a potential 'reversal' of the usual complications that arise in relation to balancing the control and benefits from testamentary trusts. Control, while important, is often uncomplicated by being given to independent professionals or family offices acting in the relevant roles.

Alternative provisions include splitting control or benefits equally between members of an eligible class, such as generations from the patriarch/matriarch, or on the age or marital status of the descendants.

One major practical consideration can be the point at which a Traditional Master Trust becomes uncommercial. For example, even a $1 billion corpus becomes only $4 million each when split over five generations of three children; even less if other forms of expenditure and allowance for inflation are taken into account. For this reason, and due to the other costs (both financial and emotional) necessary to administer a Traditional Master Trust, the structure may not present a workable solution other than for HNW and UWNW families.

Traditional master trust capital preservation

A STRATEGY USED INCREASINGLY often by all trust controllers, particularly in relation to Traditional Master Trusts, is the 'secured loan'.

For example,the Master Trust may provide funds to a beneficiary to purchase a home, on the basis that a registeredmortgage will be provided back to the Traditional Master Trust.

What happens when equity in the property increases?

If the value of the property increases, or debt to an external financier is reduced, the arrangement can often be 'topped up', by gifting further amounts,equal to the increased equity amount, to the Traditional Master Trust. It is important to note that the gift of the increased equitywill be considered a separate transaction for the purposes of bankruptcy clawback period rules.

What are the advantages of this approach?

The secured loan strategy can be conducive to an objective common to many HNW and UHNW family founders – that is, fostering financial capacity and entrepreneurial abilities in future generations of the family. This can be encouraged by allowing regulated access to the corpus of the Traditional Master Trust to assist appropriate aspirants.

Other advantages of utilising a secured loan arrangementare:

a the arrangement achieves broadly equivalent protection for the asset compared with the Traditional Master Trust retaining ownership b CGT advantages, particularly if the asset to be acquired is a main residence.

The only transaction cost should be a mortgage registration fee (although in some states, mortgage duty may also be payable).

What are the disadvantages of this approach?

The disadvantages of utilising this approach, compared withother methods of preservation are:

a the arrangement is more complex than separate ownership, and involves the preparation of additionaldocumentation (including loan agreement and security/mortgage documentation)
b it only protects the amount of net equity in the asset at the time of the loan; as mentioned above, itwill not protect increases in the asset value the individual holds
c the arrangement may be subject to the bankruptcy clawback rules.

Variations to loan arrangements

One variation, utilised by several multigenerational entrepreneurial families, avoids loans to family businesses in favour of actual ownership of the business entity itself. In these scenarios, the aspirant family member receives control of the business entity only after predetermined criteria are met, such as 'repayment' of the capital amount.

The Traditional Master Trust may be provided with a benefit, such as a share of capital growth, should the business be successful during the period of the 'loan'. This structure can work well in practice and keep the borrowing aspirant accountable to the family council or trustees throughout the process.

Chapter 6

CREATIVE USES FOR TESTAMENTARY TRUSTS

Introduction

HAVING CONSIDERED THE various types of protective and special testamentary trusts available, this chapter explores some creative uses of a testamentary trust and in particular the following:

a trust cloning
b trust splitting
c bespoke company constitutions and fettering of a trustee's discretion
d changing of domicile.

Trust cloning and trust splitting

Where assets have been built up in one trust, there is often a desire for the assets to be divided among different trusts. This mightbe for a number of reasons, including:

a to allow some assets to be controlled by certain family members and other assets to be controlled by different family members
b to separate passive investments or valuable capital assets from the risks associated with carrying on a business
c to separate multiple business activities and quarantine the risks associated with each.

Transactions of this nature can have a number of consequences, including:

a CGT on asset transfer
b stamp duty
c trust resettlement due to variations of the trust deed.

Trust cloning and splitting can offer pathways to achievinga restructure of testamentary trust assets whilst minimising adverse transaction costs.

Trust cloning is synonymous with trust 'mirroring' – that is, assets of a trust are transferred to a separate identical trust or trusts, with no changes to the meaning or effect of the trust deed. This provides for different trust estates.

In contrast, trust splitting is where the assets of the trust are split (within the same trust) so that different trustees are appointed for each part. The ability to split a trust will depend largely upon whether the trust deed includes a power to appoint a separate trustee in respect of those assets to be separated from the remaining assets.

For both cloning and splitting, care must be taken to identify the location of each asset of the trust for duty purposes, as different states have different requirements for each potential exemption.

Trust cloning

Althoughthe heyday of trust cloning ended with the abolition of the CGT 'cloning' exemption (other than in relation to certain forms of fixed trusts), trust cloning is still potentially relevant for all forms of trusts, including testamentary trusts. Although in many instances cloning itself may no longer be effective from a tax perspective, it is important to understand its history from a tax perspective and its future from a stamp duty perspective.

Cloning was (and to some extent still is) an effective tool regularly used in succession planning, asset protection and arranging finance. A properly crafted trust clone arrangement can still be effective from a Queensland duty perspective.

Cloning may be worth considering,therefore,if the tax consequences of the transfer can be otherwise managed -for example, if:

a there has not been a significant increase in the market value of the asset since it was purchased
b the small business CGT concessions in division 152 ITAA 1997 are available

c the assets to be transferred are nonCGT assets, which might otherwise be subject to duty, and the income tax consequences can be managed.

As discussed in more detail below, trust splitting does not provide the same level of asset protection as trust cloning. As a result, trust cloning mightstill be appropriate in some circumstances if the CGT consequences of cloning can be otherwise managed.

Trust splitting

The practical uses of trust splitting are broadly the same as those of trust cloning. As there are different mechanisms required for trust splitting, however, the asset protection is not as substantial as that afforded bytrust cloning.

As discussed above, trust cloning involves the establishment ofa separate, discrete trust and the transferring of assets between the two trusts.

Trust splitting, on the other hand, involves establishing a 'sub-trust' within the original trust, so that there is still only one trust, but different trustees are appointed for different assets held within that trust. The splitting of a trust does not involve a change – neither to the beneficiaries nor to the powers conferred on the trustee.

The ability to split a trust will depend on the powers provided in the trust deed (which, for most testamentary trusts, is the will) to appoint a separate trustee in respect of thoseassets that have been split.

Figure 7.1 (below) illustrates the broad structural differences between the two approaches.

Figure 6.1

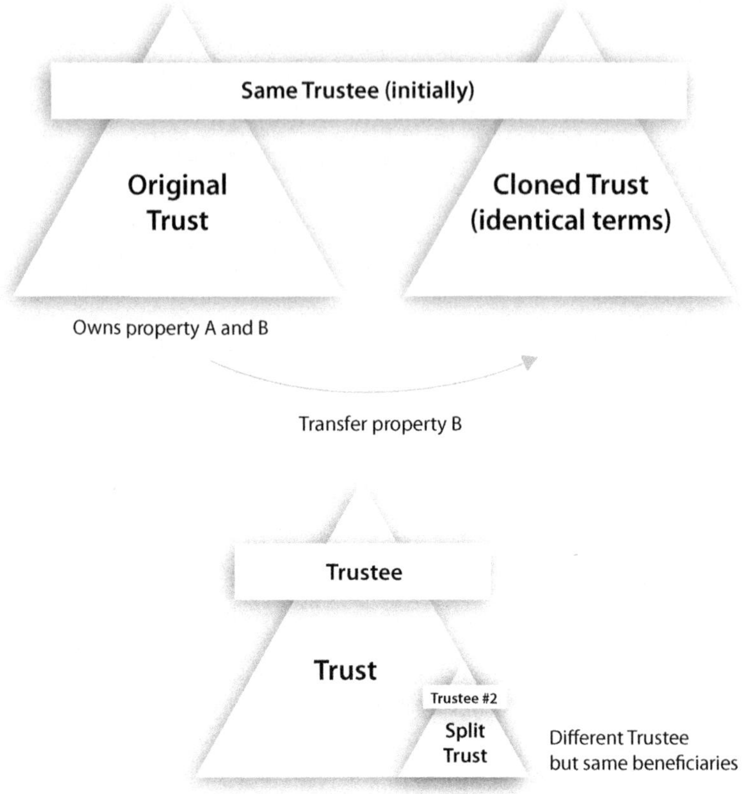

In general, trust splitting might not be ideal from a succession planning perspective, as there can be practical difficulties in relation to separating the control of the original trust and the subtrust.

In particular, the following issues, at least, would need to be addressed:

a the way in which the roles of any principal, appointor or guardian are structured under the trust deed
b the effect of any family trust election; the potential ability to make a oneoff change to a family trust election does not generally assist with trust splitting, as only one family trust election can be made for the trust as a whole

c the ability (or inability) to obtain separate tax file numbers and GST registrations for the original trust and the subtrust, if required.

In some cases, where liability and asset protection issues are not important and some ongoing cooperation amongst the trustees of the original trust and the subtrust is feasible, trust splitting can be a useful tool in succession planning.

As the assets are still held in the same trust, albeit with different trustees appointed, this effectively limits the CGT consequences of trust splitting. In particular, while there is a change of legal owner when a new trustee is appointed, the exception under the CGT rules regarding a mere change of trustee should be available.

The more difficult issue in most cases is that the terms of the will must permit splitting (that is, allowing separate trust funds) and the power to appoint more than one trustee for those separate funds.

For trusts established outside a will, it should generally be possible to insert the required powers into an existing trust deed without triggering a resettlement. This issue needs to be considered as part of a careful review of the trust deed and in the context of the ATO's position following the withdrawal of its statement of principles (SOP) on creation of a new trust (further comments in this regard are set out below).

In relation to testamentary trusts, the issues are more problematic because:

a many testamentary trusts have no variation power
b even if there is a variation power, use of it for any purpose may be invalid on public policy grounds (that is, as it allows a will maker's directions to be changed after death).

Stamp duty

In relation to the stamp duty consequences of a trust clone or trust split, the rules in each state are different – in some instances depending on the underlying assets that are to be the subject of the rearrangement.

It is therefore important to seek specialist advice before embarking on a trust clone or trust split. In broad terms:

a Queensland allows trust cloning of dutiable property without triggering stamp duty
b it is possible to perform a trust clone in New South Wales in relation to shares in a land rich company (regardless of where that company is registered). There will, however, still be marketable securities duty payable if the company is registered in New South Wales or South Australia
c other states allow some form of trust splitting to occur without triggering a stamp duty liability; however, the exact mechanisms vary, not only between jurisdictions but also depending on the underlying assets involved and the terms of the existing trust deed.

Specific comments on the taxation consequences of splitting

As noted above (other than in relation to some forms of fixed trusts) the CGT exemption on trust cloning is no longer available.

Generally CGT relief should be available on trust splitting and the basis for this is outlined in more detail below.

CGT events

The CGT events that may have potential application to a trust split are A1, E1 and E2.

CGT event A1 arises on a disposal of an asset. However, where there is a disposal as a result of a new trustee being appointed for particular assets, the exception regarding a mere change of trustee should be available.

CGT event E1 arises if a trust is created over a CGT asset. Splitting does not generally create a new declaration of trust or settlement. A new trust should not arise merely by appointing a new trustee in respect of particular assets held by the trust, and therefore CGT event E1 should not apply.

CGT event E2 occurs where an asset is transferred to a trust. With a trust split, CGT event E2 does not occur as the assets are still held in the same trust, although different trustees are appointed.

In ATO ID 2009/86, it was decided that a trust split *did* trigger CGT event E1 on the basis that there was a '*fundamental change to the rights and obligations attaching to the trust assets*'.

In these particular circumstances, there were several factors which gave rise to the ATO's conclusion that a new trust had been created, namely:

a there was a release by the original trustee of its right of indemnity against the assets transferred
b there was no right of indemnity by the new trustee against the assets which the original trustee retained
c a separate appointor was nominated for the assets transferred to the split trust
d there was a narrowing of the class of beneficiaries who could benefit from the assets transferred to the split trust, by way of a family agreement in which beneficiaries agreed to limit the distributions of the split trust to particular beneficiaries, to the exclusion of others.

In summary, the ATO gave the following reasons for its conclusion that CGT event E1 occurred:

a the trustee's rights were altered by excluding the transferred assets from its right of indemnity
b the rights of beneficiaries were altered, in that the class of persons who could benefit from the transferred assets had been narrowed.

Resettlement

Trust resettlement is an area that continues to be important for trust splitting, especially where the original trust needs to be varied before the splitting takes place.

The consequences of a resettlement include:

a all assets are treated as having been disposed of by the original trust and settled on the new trust (that is, CGT event E1 occurs)
b any losses in the trust are trapped and cannot be carried forward to offset income in the 'new' trust.

The ATO, in its SOP, provided an outline of what it believed might give rise to a resettlement of a trust. The guidance provided by the SOP indicatedthat a resettlement would arise where there has been an alteration to the trust sufficient to constitute a new trust relationship.

The SOP confirmed that a mere change of trustee does not trigger a CGT event. However, the SOP noted that '*a change in the trustee or the control of the trustee may be an element in arrangements which in their entirety amount to the creation of a new trust*'.

The ATO withdrew its SOP following the decision of the Full Court of the Federal Court of Australia in *Clark*. In that case, the trust in question was a unit trust, which had been substantially changed over several years by changing the trustee, the beneficiaries and the trust property.

In rejecting the Commissioner's argument that these amendments had amounted to a resettlement of the trust, the Court held that the three factors to consider in determining whether there has been a continuum of the trust are:

a the terms of the trust deed (which as noted above, are normally set out in a will for testamentary trusts)
b the trust property
c the membership of the trust.

Further, the Court confirmed that where the changes are within the scope of the variation power in the relevant trust deed, changes over time to the trust property and beneficiaries should not trigger a resettlement, provided that they can be identified at all times and there has not been a severance which would lead to the termination of the trust.

Following the withdrawal of its SOP, the ATO releasedTax Determination 2012/21. This determination states the ATO's position, formerly set out in its SOP, was unsustainable following the Court's decision in *Clark* and that:

'Neither CGT event E1 nor CGT event E2 ... happens unless:

- *the change causes the existing trust to terminate and a new trust to arise for trust law purposes, or*
- *the effect of the change ... is such as to lead to a particular asset being subject to a separate charter of rights and obligations such as to give rise to the conclusion that that asset has been settled on terms of a different trust.'*

Following the Court's decision in *Clark* and the subsequent removal of the ATO's SOP, the risk of a resettlement on a trust split has clearly been reduced.

When structuring asplitting transaction, however, it is arguably still the case that:

a the trustee indemnity provisions should be retained
b no steps should be taken towards limiting the range of beneficiaries entitled to the assets of the trust and, in particular:
   (i) no steps should be taken by particular beneficiaries to renounce their entitlements in respect of the assets held in the split trust or the original trust
   (ii) no agreements should be made in respect of future distributions from the split trust or the original trust – that is, the trustee of each trust should retain full discretion as to distributions in each year

c the trust deed should contain an express power permitting a separate trustee to be appointed to particular trust assets. As set out above, for testamentary trusts, this aspect may be particularly difficult to address, unless the relevant powers are in the will before the will maker dies.

Bespoke trustee company constitutions

ONE OF THE critical aspects of any estate planning exercise is determining what assets will, in fact, form part of the personal wealth to be distributed under a will.

Set out below are specific comments in relation to the way in which personally owned assets can be controlled via tailored trustee company constitutions, where those companies are appointed as trustees for a testamentary trust.

Virtually all of the comments are equally applicable to similar control mechanisms for preexisting discretionary trusts. Therefore, although the focus of this book is on testamentary trusts, many of the principles are likely to be relevant for similar trust structures established during a will maker's lifetime.

Control of testamentary trusts

The control of a testamentary trust will usually rest within two key roles, namely:

a the trustee
b the appointor (again sometimes referred to as the principal, guardian, nominator or protector), if such a position exists.

The transfer of control of a testamentary trust can generally be achievedby:

a providing for the succession of the role of appointor or individual trustee (if applicable) and, in this regard, it is imperative to review the terms of the willin order to ensure that control of the trust passes to the intended and appropriate successor or successors
b transferring the shares in a corporate trustee (including the possibility of a share split in the corporate trustee)
c careful drafting of the constitution or shareholders' agreement (if one exists) of the corporate trustee (where applicable).

'Corporatising' a discretionary trust

It is possible to provide for quasi corporatisation of a testamentary trust by appointing a corporate trustee and implementing a number of control mechanisms in the governing documentation of the company – for example, a shareholders' agreement or bespoke company constitution.

It is generally accepted that it is not possible for a beneficiary of a testamentary trust to prescribe how the trustee can exercise its discretion, as this will contravene the fundamental principle of trust law – which is that the discretion of a trustee of a discretionary trust cannot be fettered.

However, it is possible to utilise the rules in the Corporations Act,as they apply to the corporate trustee, to implement a specific framework within which the trustee can operate. This framework is often outlined in the constitution for the corporate trustee, or in a shareholders' agreement, which will often operate in conjunction with an interfamily agreement or a family constitution.

By inserting control mechanisms in the governing documents for a corporate trustee, it is possible to create specific levels of control over the trust and to ensure that the controllers of the trust exercise their discretion in a manner which is consistent with the family succession strategy.

Corporations Act

The Corporations Act provides that a company's constitution is a contract between the directors and the company (that is, the members).

Section 136(2) Corporations Act permits a constitution to impose additional obligations on directors and members, in addition to the requirements set out in the Corporations Act, provided that the constitution only varies the replaceable rules.

Generally, the control mechanisms for the director and for decision-making, which are 'hardwired' into a bespoke constitution, will only alter the replaceable rules, and therefore should be valid under the Corporations Act.

Further, the sections in the Corporations Act governing the transfer of shares are also replaceable rules, and therefore any requirements in a constitution confirming (for example) that a member may only transfer their shares to their lineal descendants will be valid under the Corporations Act.

Examples of control mechanisms which may be appropriate to include in a bespoke trustee company constitution:

a specifying how shareholder and director decisions should be made – including, for example, that particular decisions may only be made by unanimous or special majority decision
b a requirement that each shareholder should be entitled to appoint and remove a representative director
c restrictions on the transfer of shares
d restrictions on the class of people entitled to be a shareholder or a director – for example, shareholders must be lineal descendants of nominated family members
e naming of specific successor directors upon the occurrence of specified events
f the involvement of any independent (non-family) advisers in the management of the company and the extent of their involvement
g any triggers for the transition of control to particular people – for example, on family members reaching a specified age.

Achieving certainty in relation to distributions of wealth (trust distributions) is often an important part of the family succession strategy and can be addressed in a number of ways – for example:

a. inserting a distribution policy into an interfamily agreement or a family constitution, shareholders' agreement or constitution – for example, formulas or specific guidelines
b. leaving discretion to the controllers of the wealth, but requiring that decisions in this regard be made unanimously, with reference to the guidance that is provided by, for example, a family council or professional advisers.

It is also necessary to ensure that the appointor roles align with the control mechanisms implemented for the corporate trustee. In some circumstances, it might be appropriate for the appointor provisions to be removed completely in order to centralise control with the corporate trustee, determined by its shareholding. In other circumstances, it might be appropriate to retain the appointor role and ensure that the succession of this role is 'hardwired' into the terms of the will.

Where there are joint appointors, it is important to review the decision-making mechanisms and to ensure that they align with the approach implemented at the trustee level. Where the appointor is a natural person it is critical to understand how the will provides for the succession of this role on that person's death or incapacity.

Domicile

As mentioned earlier in this chapter, stamp duty exemption from a true 'cloning' perspective is only available in Queensland.

South Australia is unique as it is currently the only Australian jurisdiction that has effectively abolished the rule against perpetuities.

Whether or not the controllers of a testamentary trust can 'forum shop' the jurisdiction that they wish to be subject to, is an area of some uncertainty.

The main issues that need to be considered are:

a it is generally accepted that in order for a trustee to change the relevant jurisdiction, it must have the power to do so under the trust instrument

b as mentioned above, given that many testamentary trusts do not have any power to vary, this may in a practical sense, prevent a change of relevant law

c in relation to the changing of jurisdiction to South Australia for perpetuity periods, in addition to the variation to change the relevant law, it would also be necessary, in most testamentary trust instruments, to formally amend the vesting date definition; this might be prohibited for the reasons outlined above

d even if a testamentary trust has a power to vary, it may be that a purported attempt to change the relevant law is held to be invalid on public policy grounds or, alternatively, due to the various rules prohibiting the delegation of testamentary powers

e there remains some residual risk, despite the *Clark* decision, that any change of relevant law may of itself (or when combined with other changes) constitute a resettlement for CGT purposes of the trust

f depending on the underlying assets of the relevant trust, any purported change to the relevant law might not provide the intended benefits. For example, if there is a desire to transfer real property under a trust clone and that real property is located outside Queensland, even if the testamentary trust is regulated by Queensland laws there will still be an obligation to arrange for stamping in the jurisdiction where the property is physically located
g this said, the practical restrictions on changing jurisdiction might not be as problematic in relation to trusts seeking to be subject to South Australian law for perpetuity purposes, although the issue in this regard remains largely untested.

Conclusion

IN MANY RESPECTS, the ability to use creative planning for testamentary trusts is analogous to similar strategies for any other form of trust.

There are, however, some fundamental differences in the way testamentary trusts can be adjusted. It is therefore critical to adopt a methodical approach that addresses all potential issues.

Given the increasing prevalence of testamentary trusts in the estate planning process and the massive amount of wealth that is likely to be subject to intergenerational transfer over the next 20 years, the planning opportunities in relation to testamentary trusts will, in all likelihood, only continue to become increasingly important.

Chapter 7

THE TAXATION OF TESTAMENTARY TRUSTS

Introduction

HAVING CONSIDERED THE advantages and various structuring alternatives for a testamentary trust, this chapter will focus on the taxation implications of using testamentary trusts under an estate plan. Specifically, the chapter will address:

a distributions from testamentary trusts, including:
   (i) distributions to minor beneficiaries
   (ii) external accretions to testamentary trusts after death
   (iii) the treatment of capital gains
b implications of holding a main residence in a testamentary trust
c the transfer of assets from:
   (i) the will maker to the LPR
   (ii) the LPR to the testamentary trust
   (iii) the testamentary trust to a beneficiary during the term of the trust and on vesting.

Distributions

MOST TESTAMENTARY TRUSTS provide the trustee with flexibility to allocate income and capital with reference to the facts at the time, rather than to a will maker's prediction (no matter how careful) of the future. In doing so, the testamentary trust allows the trustee to make a greater distribution for the will maker's children with special needs, such as (in particular) wastrel children, as well as those with a disability.

A testamentary trust can be drafted such that it complies with the requirements set out in section 102AG(2)(a)(i)ITAA 1936, so that,each year, income allocated to minor children is not subject to the same tax rates as if it were a normal family discretionary trust established during a person's lifetime (where the first $400 distributed to a child is tax free but then any further income is taxed at the highest rate which could be up to 66%).

Where income is derived under the section quoted above, the income is treated as 'excepted trust income' and infant children are assessed at the normal, individual rates (the first $24,000 (approximately) tax free and the balance at normal adult rates, with a higher tax free amount available where the low income tax offset is available). This might be a significant saving in tax when considering the gross income for a family unit.

The Commissioner has some discretion in these cases, but generally it is exercised in favour of testamentary trusts as they are a 'traditional' form of trust.

Furthermore, it is generally accepted that testamentary trusts provide scope for tax planning opportunities, provided the arrangements entered into are capable of being characterised as arm's length dealings (albeit that the parties involved may not necessarily be at arm's length).

For example, income from an arrangement involving a testamentary trust that increases its income earning ability by borrowing on an arm's length basis would still fall within Division 6AA ITAA 1936, whereas income from gifts or distributions from other 'related' individuals or entities would not.

The specific questions that are often raised, in the context of the tax planning opportunities under Division 6AA, are:

a is excepted trust income limited to that income which derives from property held by the deceased at the date of their death? In other words, must the underlying capital assets always remain the same or can these assets be disposed of and new assets acquired within the trust structure, and would income from new assets enjoy the excepted status?

b assuming that the underlying capital assets can be changed, what (if any), limitations are placed on the types of changes that can take place and, in particular, can the total capital value of the trust be increased, by way of:

  (i) a testamentary trust going to a bank and borrowing money and then utilising this money in addition to its existing capital to purchase new assets? If so, can all of the income from the asset acquired both with existing testamentary trust money and a loan from a bank enjoy excepted trust income status or does some sort of apportionment need to take place?

  (ii) distributions made from other trusts to a testamentary trust thereby increasing the capital available for investment via a testamentary trust with all income from this new investment enjoying the excepted trust income rates?

  (iii) a beneficiary of a testamentary trust gifting money to a testamentary trust?

c if income is originally sourced from a testamentary trust but is thendistributed, via a trust established prior to death, to an infant beneficiary, does it retain its status as excepted trust income?

Each of these issues will be dealt with in turn. In all of these situations it would be necessary to consider the specific anti-avoidance provisions set out in Div 6AA, and the general anti-avoidance provisions set out in Part IVA.These provisions,however, are outside the scope of this book.

Is Division 6AA limited to income derived from estate assets?

SUBSECTIONS 102AG(2)(A)(I) AND 102AG(2)(d)(i) of Division 6AA ITAA 1936 make it clear the provisions are not limited to income derived from estate assets.

Under section 102AG(2)(a)(i), excepted trust income is the amount that is assessable income of a trust estate that resulted from a will, codicil or court order varying a will or codicil.

Importantly, the subsection only prescribes how the trust estate is deemed to have arisen and does not place any limitations on the management of the trust estate, or on the assets which the trust may hold.

The fact that estate assets forming part of the trust estate may be realised and others may be acquired has no implications for the validity of a testamentary trust, or for the ability of the trustee of a testamentary trust to treat the income as excepted. Similarly, if the trustee decides to borrow money and acquire assets which earn income, then Div 6AA applies to that income.

What limitations might be imposed

Section 102AG(3) ITAA 1936 contains an exception for non-arm's length arrangements. In particular, it provides that, if any two or more parties to:

a the derivation of the excepted trust income mentioned in subsection (2) or
b any act or transaction directly or indirectly connected with the derivation of that excepted trust income

were not dealing with each other at arm's length in relation to the derivation of income, or in relation to the act or transaction, the excepted trust income is only so much (if any) of that income as would have been derived if they had been dealing with each other at arm's length in relation to the derivation, or in relation to the act or transaction.

Essentially, this means that if, for instance, the loan was not at arm's length, but at a more favourable interest rate compared with the market, then the income derived would have been less, and therefore the amount which can be treated as excepted trust income is reduced.

The case of *The Trustee for the Estate of the late AW Furse No. 5 Will Trust v FCT* 91 ATC 4007 is one of the few reported decisions dealing with Div 6AA.

In this case, a will made in July 1974, shortly before the will maker passed away, established multiple testamentary trusts, each for a capital of $1. A trustee was then appointed over one of the testamentary trusts and proceeded to borrow small amounts of money and acquire a unit in a unit trust.

The ATO did not consider the income from the unit as excepted income and argued that the income derived by the trustee was not assessable income of a trust estate that 'resulted from a will'.

Hill J rejected the ATO's argument and held that it was only necessary that the parties be dealing on an arm's length basis and that it was not necessary that they be arm's length parties.

The Court noted that, provided the trust estate was created by a will and the arm's length test applied, then any income of a testamentary trust would be considered as excepted trust income.

A secondary issue,which was not explored by the ATO, was the potential for a Part IVA argument, given the circumstances where the will maker,shortly before his death, created a will establishing a number of testamentary trusts with nominal capital.

Will makers and trustees mustensure, therefore, when establishing testamentary trusts under a will, that the arrangement does not fall within the anti-avoidance provisions.

An additional consideration is that, unless the trustee gives arm's length consideration for the payment, income from distributions by trusts established prior to death will not enjoy excepted trust income status because the parties are not dealing at arm's length. Testamentary trust distributions to an infant beneficiary via *inter vivos* trust

Where there is a distribution of income from a testamentary trust to an *inter vivos* trust, and then to an infant beneficiary, the better view appears to be that the distribution does not have the status of excepted trust income.

Section 102AG(1) ITAA 1936 requires that a trust have a prescribed person – essentially an infant, subject to certain exceptions in 102AC(2) – as a beneficiary. Although it could be argued that a testamentary trust has, as its ultimate beneficiary, an infant, and although 102AG(1) does not expressly exclude an indirect interest as a beneficiary, 102AG(1) is likely to be construed as dealing only with direct beneficiaries of a testamentary trust.

Having said this, there is an argument that the income of the 'trust estate', contemplated in the opening words to 102AG(2), need not be the same trust estate, and that the income received by an infant beneficiary via an existing family trust is excepted trust income *'in relation to a beneficiary of the trust estate (that is the family trust) to the extent to which the amount – (a) is assessable income of a trust estate (that is the testamentary trust) that resulted from – (i) a will'.*

Distributions following Bamford

One of the critical outcomes of the High Court's decision in *Bamford* is the determination of the meaning of the term 'income' under section 97 ITAA 1936. As has been well documented, the High Court concluded that in determining the 'income of the trust estate' for the purposes of section 97, consideration needs to be given to the deed, rather than the ordinary concept of income.

In the context of a testamentary trust, the terms of the deed are set out under the will.

Support for this position was garnered from, amongst other sources, the distinct wording incorporated within section 97 ITAA 1936 between 'income of the trust estate' and 'net income of the trust estate'.

Practically, therefore, all testamentary trust wills must incorporate powers for a trustee to determine what is and what is not included as income for the trust. Amongst other things, this should include the ability for the trustee to determine whether or not to include net or gross capital gains as trust income.

While this should be possible for newly crafted testamentary trust wills, careful reviews should be undertaken for any testamentary trusts established under deceased estates.

The other main component of the decision in *Bamford* related to the appointment of trust distributions to beneficiaries. The High Court considered the meaning of the term 'share' for the purposes of section 97 ITAA 1936.

A 'percentage' approach simply assigns a set proportion or percentage of the income to individual beneficiaries. In contrast, a 'fixed amount' approach involves the trustee resolving to appoint a fixed amount of income to an individual beneficiary.

For example, fixing the amount of the distribution of income for two of three beneficiaries of the trust, with the remaining being distributed to the third beneficiary, means that any increase or decrease in assessable income would only affect the distribution to the third beneficiary.

The High Court in *Bamford* held that 'share', in the context of section 97, referred to the proportionate entitlement of each beneficiary to the income of the trust estate. Therefore, it is the proportion that determines the amount of assessable income that is attributed to the beneficiary, even if fixed amounts have been appointed to the beneficiaries under the trust. As a result of the High Court's decision in *Bamford*, there should not be any particular concern for distributions out of testamentary trusts,assuming that trustee resolutions (or minutes) are appropriately crafted in the context of that decision.

Having said this, there is potential for significant adverse consequences to arisein relation to a testamentary trust where the income and capital beneficiaries are different.A classic example of this would be a 'lineal descendant' testamentary trust, where the income beneficiaries are crafted far more widely than the capital beneficiaries

Furthermore, in situations where atestamentary trust already exists because the will maker has died, the relevant parties must ensure thatthe will does in fact have the requisite powers as, generallyspeaking, it is impossible to amend the trust instrument following the death of the will maker.

Family trust elections and interposed entity elections

It is important to keep in mind the consequences of a trustee making a family trust election or interposed entity election. These elections may apply to any form of trust, including discretionary and unit trusts as well as testamentary trusts.

In particular, where such an election has been made, despite what might otherwise be provided for in the trust instrument, the election will effectively limit the range of potential beneficiaries who can receive a distribution without triggering a penal tax consequence (that is, the family trust distribution tax).

A trustee will generally make a family trust election for one or more of the following reasons:

a to access franking credits
b to be able to utilise prior year losses and bad debt deductions
c to simplify the continuity of ownership test
d to eliminate the need to comply with the trustee beneficiary reporting rules .

A family trust election is made in accordance to section 272-80 ITAA 1936, which requires that a 'test individual' be specified, around whose family will benefit from all future distributions.

A test individual's family will broadly include, under section 272-95 ITAA 1936, the immediate family of the test individual and their spouse, as well as the lineal descendants of the immediate family.

Once a family trust election has been made, the trust will be restricted to making distributions to trust beneficiaries within the family group. Failure to do so will incur family trust distribution tax being imposed at a flat rate of 47%, which is payable by the distributing trust within 21 days after distribution is made.

Likewise, an interposed entity election for a company, trust or partnership in a test individual's family group may be made where income is intended to be distributed to that entity from a trust that has a family trust election in place.

In order to be eligible to make an interposed entity election, a 'family control test' must be satisfied, as set out under section 272-87 ITAA 1936.

Main residences

Generally, a main residence will be either exempt or fully exempt from CGT on its disposal. This position is effectively maintained where a property was the main residence of a deceased person immediately prior to their death.

The two key rules are:

a if a property was exempt under the main residence exemption before the death of the deceased owner, and a beneficiary moves into the dwelling and it becomes that beneficiary's main residence, the main residence exemption will continue to be fully available

b if a beneficiary sells the dwelling within 24 months of the date of death of the deceased person whose main residence the dwelling was, whether or not that beneficiary resides in the property, the property will be exempt from CGT (under what is known as 'the 24-month rule').

Where assets are held as joint tenants, the surviving joint tenant is treated as if the dwelling had passed to the surviving owner 'as a beneficiary in a deceased estate' (section 118-197 ITAA 1997).

The calculation of the 24-month period will be from the date of death until settlement of the disposal, rather than until the exchange of contracts.

It should be noted that under section 118-195 ITAA 1997, it does not matter that the dwelling was not the deceased's main residence, or it was used for income-producing purposes, for a period of time during their ownership. The only requirement is that the dwelling was the deceased's main residence just before their death and was not being used for income-producing purposes at that time.

Main residence exemption and testamentary trusts

As outlined above, the CGT main residence exemption in section 118-195 ITAA 1997 will apply to capital gains made in relation to dwellings owned by individuals whose interest in the dwelling was passed to them as 'a beneficiary in a deceased estate, or as trustee of a deceased estate'. A 'trustee of a deceased estate' would include only the LPR and not a testamentary trust trustee.

Unfortunately, there is no statement from the ATO similar to that in PS LA 2003/12 (which applies only to Division 128 ITAA 1997), confirming that a testamentary trust trustee will be treated the same as an LPR for the purposes of Division 118 ITAA 1997.

Therefore, the only way to be certain that the main residence exemption under section 118-195 ITAA 1997 will apply is to ensure either that:

a the property is disposed of by either the LPR or an individual beneficiary (that is, without passing to a testamentary trust) within 24 months of the date of death of the deceased or

b the deceased's main residence does not pass to a testamentary trust with the remainder of the estate assets and is instead passed directly to an individual beneficiary as owner, and to have the deceased's spouse, or a person with a right to occupy, live in the house as their main residence.

However, it would be open to argument that, if a deceased's main residence passed to an individual testamentary trust trustee, who then held that property on trust solely for the benefit of either:

a the deceased's spouse, or

b a person with a right to occupy the house under the deceased's will,

and those persons did occupy the dwelling as their main residence, the exemption would remain available to the testamentary trust trustee on a subsequent disposal of the dwelling.

In practice, it is often the case that,where a main residence is involved, multiple testamentary trusts are established. One (or more) testamentary trust would be established to hold the residuary estate and would generally have a wide range of beneficiaries.

An additional testamentary trust would then be established to hold only the main residence of the deceased. The beneficiaries of the testamentary trust would be limited to:

a the deceased's spouse, or
b a person with a right to occupy the house under the deceased's will.

It is vital that, if a person other than the deceased's spouse is to live in the dwelling, that person is given the right to occupy the house under the terms of the will.

Main residence – partial exemptions

The general rules about absences from a main residence are set out in section 118-45 ITAA 1997 and apply equally in deceased estate cases and in the case of disposals during a person's lifetime.

The general rule for post-CGT dwellings is that the exemption is pro-rated by reference to the number of days that were non-main resident days, of both the deceased and the beneficiary (or LPR), over the total ownership period of the dwelling by the deceased and the beneficiary (section 118-125 ITAA 97).

Section 118-200 ITAA 1997 sets out a partial exemption for a beneficiary or LPR where the full main residence exemption under section 118-195 is unable to be accessed. The partial exemption will generally apply in situations where:

a a beneficiary did not occupy the dwelling for their entire ownership period, commencing from the date of death of the deceased, where the dwelling was either a pre-CGT asset of the deceased or was the deceased's main residence immediately prior to their death b although the dwelling has been the beneficiary's main residence for the entire period since the time of death of the deceased, it was not the main residence of the deceased just before the deceased's death.

Where a dwelling or family home has been used for income-producing purposes by either the deceased or a beneficiary or legal personal representative, a partial exemption may apply where the income-producing activity does not constitute the entire usage of the dwelling. These exemptions are set out in sections 118-190 and 118-92 ITAA 1997 and will not be discussed in further detail in this book.

Transfer of assets

Upon the death of a will-maker, each asset of the estate will potentially be transferred three times:

a from the will maker to the LPR
b from the LPR to the beneficiary of the estate, which may be the trustee of a testamentary trust
c from the testamentary trust to a beneficiary, either as a capital distribution during the lifetime of the trust or as a distribution of corpus upon vesting.

The CGT consequences of each transfer above must be separately considered.

Distributions from will maker to LPR

The first rollover to examine is the initial transfer of a deceased's assets from the deceased person to their LPR for distribution under the terms of the deceased's will.

As a starting point, the general position is that, when a taxpayer dies, any capital gain or loss from any event relating to a CGT asset owned by the deceased is disregarded under section 128-10 ITAA 1997. This means that the distribution from the deceased to their LPR does not result in a CGT liability for the deceased and there are effectively no other CGT consequences for the deceased.

As to the consequences to the LPR, the CGT assets are taken, under section 128-15 ITAA 1997, to have been acquired by the LPR on the date the deceased died. The cost base of the CGT asset (other than for a property which was a main residence for the deceased immediately before they died, which is discussed below) for the LPR is modified under 128-15(4) ITAA 1997 so that:

a for pre-CGT assets in the hands of the deceased, the first element of the LPR's cost base (and reduced cost base) is the market value of the asset on the day the deceased died -meaning that pre-CGT assets in the hands of the deceased become post-CGT assets in the hands of the LPR
b for post-CGT assets in the hands of the deceased, the first element of the LPR's cost base (and reduced cost base) is the deceased's costs base (or reduced costs base) at the date of their death – meaning that the deceased effectively passes their cost base and reduced cost base to the LPR.

Distributions from LPR to testamentary trusts

From a CGT perspective, a testamentary trust is treated in much the same way as other trusts. However, it should be noted that CGT event E1 (section 104-55 ITAA 1997 – Creating a trust over a CGT asset) does not apply to a testamentary trust, since that event only applies to the creation of a trust 'by declaration or settlement'. In the testamentary trust scenario, there is no such declaration of trust and there is no initial settlement sum.

The CGT rules thatapply to the distribution from the deceased to the LPR apply equally to subsequent distributions from the LPR to a 'beneficiary'. It would appear that 'beneficiary' for the purposes of the ITAA 1997 includes the trustee of a testamentary trust (however, as shown later in this chapter, for the purpose of Division 128 the ATO treats the trustee of a testamentary trust in the same way that it treats an LPR).

A CGT asset is taken to have passed to a beneficiary of a deceased's estate if the beneficiary (or, in this case, the trustee of the testamentary trust) becomes the owner of the asset, whether under the terms of:

a the deceased's will
b under the intestacy laws, or
c under a deed of arrangement – section 128-20 ITAA 1997.

As with the initial transfer from the deceased to the LPR, on a subsequent distribution from the LPR to a testamentary trust, any capital gain or loss that the LPR (rather than the deceased) makes is disregarded (although this time, the relevant provision is found in section 128-14(3) ITAA 1997, rather than in section 128-10 ITAA 1997).

Again, the testamentary trust trustee is taken to have acquired the CGT assets of the deceased at the date of the deceased's death (rather than the date on which they were distributed by the LPR) and the first element of the cost base (and reduced cost base) for the testamentary trust trustee will be:

a for pre-CGT assets in the hands of the deceased, the market value of the asset on the day the deceased died
b for post-CGT assets in the hands of the deceased, the deceased's costs base (or reduced cost base) at the date of their death (section 128-15(3) ITAA 1997).

The testamentary trust trustee is also able to include in its cost base any expenditure the LPR has incurred, up to the time of the disposal by the LPR, that the LPR would have been entitled to include in its cost base, had it retained the asset (section 128-15(5) ITAA 1997).

Distributions from testamentary trusts

In 2003, the ATO released PS LA 2003/12,which states that its purpose is to inform ATO staff that the Commissioner will not depart from the long-standing administrative practice of treating the trustee of a testamentary trust in the same way that an LPR is treated for the purposes of Division 128 (and in particular section 128-15(3) ITAA 1997).

This is generally accepted to mean that there is an exemption from CGT covering the 'transfer' from the LPR to the trustee of the testamentary trust in the first instance as well as the subsequent transfer to an eventual beneficiary of the estate.

This subsequent transfer may either involve a capital distribution being made by the trustee of the trust to a beneficiary during the lifetime of the trust, or a payment of capital upon vesting of the trust.

The result of PS LA 2003/12 is that, on the subsequent disposal of a CGT asset from a testamentary trust trustee to a beneficiary of the testamentary trust:

a any capital gain or loss that the testamentary trust trustee makes is disregarded under section 128-15 (3) ITAA 1997, and
b the beneficiary will be taken to have acquired the CGT assets of the deceased at the date of the deceased's death (rather than at the date on which they were distributed by the LPR) and the first element of the cost base and reduced cost base for the beneficiary will be:
   (i) for pre-CGT assets in the hands of the deceased, the market value of the asset on the day the deceased died
   (ii) for post-CGT assets in the hands of the deceased, the deceased's cost base (or reduced cost base) at the date of their death (section 128-15(3) ITAA 1997).

Ultimately, PS LA 2003/12, sections 128 – in particular sections 128(2), (3) and (4) ITAA 1997 – effectively apply twice:

a initially, when the LPR is the 'LPR' for the purposes of Division 128 and the testamentary trust trustee is the 'beneficiary'
b subsequently, when the testamentary trust trustee is treated as an 'LPR' for the purposes of Division 128 and the beneficiaries of the testamentary trust are treated as the 'beneficiaries'.

CGT event K3

The Commissioner has noted that the position in PS LA 2003/12 is subject to CGT event K3, which covers assets passing to tax-advantaged entities. CGT event K3 operates to ensure that, where assets pass to concessional taxed entities from a deceased estate, a capital gain or loss is recognised in the deceased's final tax return, preventing assets with embedded capital gains from avoiding capital gains when they are later disposed of by the concessionally taxed entity.

CGT event K3 has, in the past, been avoided by ensuring that an asset does not pass to a concessionally taxed entity until after the deceased's standard amendment period (generally four years after the assessment) has expired.

As part of the 2011-12 Budget measures, it was announced that amendments would be made to ensure that, where CGT event K3 happened outside of the deceased's standard amendment period, a CGT liability would still arise in the deceased's tax return. It was proposed this could be achieved by excluding CGT event K3 from the standard amendment period.

In particular, the CGT event would have been deemed to happen to the relevant entity that passed the asset to the concessionally taxed entity (rather than yothe beneficiary), avoiding the need to amend the deceased's tax return.

This change would have allowed the entity to which CGT event K3 applied to be able to utilise their realised capital losses against CGT event K3, instead of the deceased estate utilising the wil makers' capital losses against the capital gain from CGT event K3.

The change would also have been consistent with how Division 128 operates under PS LA 2003/12 where an LPR or testamentary trust trustee sells an asset to a third party, rather than passing the asset to the intended beneficiary of the estate.

However, as with other proposed changes mentioned below, the announced changes to CGT event K3 were abandoned in late 2013.

Legislating CGT exemption for testamentary trust distribution of asset

In the 2011-12and 2012-13Federal Budgets, it was proposed that the current ATO practice set out in PS LA 2003/12 and allowing a testamentary trust to distribute an asset of a deceased person without a CGT taxing point occurring, would be codified.

Whilst draft legislation to effect the change was prepared, the 2013 Liberal Federal Government announced that it was reviewing the progress of a large number of unenacted legislative announcements and ultimately confirmed the amendments above would not be implemented.

In 2014, the ATO confirmed it will continue to adopt the approach set out in PS LA 2003/12.

Where an intended beneficiary dies before administration is completed

In June 2012, the Federal Government released a proposals paper 'Minor amendments to the capital gains tax law', whichspecifically addressed the circumstance where the intended beneficiary dies before administration of an estate is completed.

Generally, in that situation, section 128-15 ITAA 1997 provides a CGT rollover, provided that the asset passes from the first deceased's LPR to the beneficiary's LPR.

However, no CGT rollover exists where the asset passes (ultimately) from the first deceased's LPR via the second deceased's LPR to the trustee of a testamentary trust or a beneficiary of the intended beneficiary's (the second deceased) estate because the asset was not one that the intended beneficiary owned when they died.

The Labor Federal Government, in power until July 2013, proposed the introduction of measures to allow the intended beneficiary's LPR to access the rollover where the intended beneficiary dies before an asset that the first deceased owned passes to them, regardless of whether it passes first to a testamentary trust trustee.

Again, however, the 2013 Liberal Federal Government confirmed the amendments would not be proceeding.

Conclusion

IN CONCLUSION, PROVIDED a will is structured properly, the use of testamentary trusts can effectively defer the CGT taxing point until the eventual disposal of a CGT asset by a testamentary trust beneficiary (rather than the CGT taxing point occurring on the distribution of the CGT asset from the testamentary trust to the beneficiary).

It is however important that the LPR and testamentary trust trustees are aware that they should not dispose of assets under a power of sale to a beneficiary,as this will bring forward the CGT taxing point, with-the tax imposed on the LPR or testamentary trust trustee.

The deferral of the CGT taxing point for testamentary trusts effectively mirrors the CGT position on the administration of estates without testamentary trusts, where the CGT taxing point is again the disposal of the CGT asset by the beneficiary. However, the use of testamentary trusts provides significant tax planning and asset protection advantages over a distribution directly from an LPR to a beneficiary.

It is also vital that, where main residences are concerned, a will is correctly structured to ensure the best possible chance of maintaining access to the CGT main residence exemption.

Printed in Dunstable, United Kingdom

91343650R00117